How to Be a Stoic

Translated by Robert Dobbin,
C.D.N. Costa and Martin Hammond

PENGUIN BOOKS — GREAT IDEAS

PENGUIN BOOKS

UK | USA | Canada | Ireland | Australia
India | New Zealand | South Africa

Penguin Books is part of the Penguin Random House group
of companies whose addresses can be found at
global.penguinrandomhouse.com.

Penguin
Random House
UK

Taken from *Discourses and Selected Writings* (Penguin Classics 2008),
Dialogues and Letters (Penguin Classics, 2005) and *Meditations*
(Penguin Classics 2006)
This selection published in Penguin Books 2020

003

Translations copyright © Robert Dobbin, 2008; C.D.N. Costa, 2005;
Martin Hammond, 2006

Set in 11.2/13.75 pt Dante MT Std
Typeset by Jouve (UK), Milton Keynes
Printed and bound in Great Britain by Clays Ltd, Elcograf S.p.A.

A CIP catalogue record for this book
is available from the British Library

ISBN: 978-0-241-47526-3

Contents

Enchiridion – Epictetus   1

On the Shortness of Life – Seneca   31

Meditations – Marcus Aurelius   65

Enchiridion

CHAPTER I

[1] We are responsible for some things, while there are others for which we cannot be held responsible. The former include our judgement, our impulse, our desire, aversion and our mental faculties in general; the latter include the body, material possessions, our reputation, status – in a word, anything not in our power to control. [2] The former are naturally free, unconstrained and unimpeded, while the latter are frail, inferior, subject to restraint – and none of our affair.

[3] Remember that if you mistake what is naturally inferior for what is sovereign and free, and what is not your business for your own, you'll meet with disappointment, grief and worry and be at odds with God and man. But if you have the right idea about what really belongs to you and what does not, you will never be subject to force or hindrance, you will never blame or criticize anyone, and everything you do will be done willingly. You won't have a single rival, no one to hurt you, because you will be proof against harm of any kind.

[4] With rewards this substantial, be aware that a

casual effort is not sufficient. Other ambitions will have to be sacrificed, altogether or at least for now. If you want these rewards at the same time that you are striving for power and riches, chances are you will not get to be rich and powerful while you aim for the other goal; and the rewards of freedom and happiness will elude you altogether.

[5] So make a practice at once of saying to every strong impression: 'An impression is all you are, not the source of the impression.' Then test and assess it with your criteria, but one primarily: ask, 'Is this something that is, or is not, in my control?' And if it's not one of the things that you control, be ready with the reaction, 'Then it's none of my concern.'

CHAPTER 2

[1] The faculty of desire purports to aim at securing what you want, while aversion purports to shield you from what you don't. If you fail in your desire, you are unfortunate, if you experience what you would rather avoid you are unhappy. So direct aversion only towards things that are under your control and alien to your nature, and you will not fall victim to any of the things that you dislike. But if your resentment is directed at illness, death or poverty, you are headed for disappointment.

[2] Remove it from anything not in our power to control, and direct it instead toward things contrary to our nature that we do control. As for desire, suspend it

completely for now. Because if you desire something outside your control, you are bound to be disappointed; and even things we do control, which under other circumstances would be deserving of our desire, are not yet within our power to attain. Restrict yourself to choice and refusal; and exercise them carefully, with discipline and detachment.

CHAPTER 3

In the case of particular things that delight you, or benefit you, or to which you have grown attached, remind yourself of what they are. Start with things of little value. If it is china you like, for instance, say, 'I am fond of a piece of china.' When it breaks, then you won't be as disconcerted. When giving your wife or child a kiss, repeat to yourself, 'I am kissing a mortal.' Then you won't be so distraught if they are taken from you.

CHAPTER 4

Whenever planning an action, mentally rehearse what the plan entails. If you are heading out to bathe, picture to yourself the typical scene at the bathhouse – people splashing, pushing, yelling and pinching your clothes. You will complete the act with more composure if you say at the outset, 'I want a bath, but at the same time I want to keep my will aligned with nature.' Do it with every act. That way if something occurs to spoil your bath, you will have ready the thought, 'Well, this was not my only intention, I also meant to keep my will in line with nature – which is impossible if I go all to pieces whenever anything bad happens.'

CHAPTER 5

It is not events that disturb people, it is their judgements concerning them. Death, for example, is nothing frightening, otherwise it would have frightened Socrates. But the judgement that death is frightening – now, that is something to be afraid of. So when we are frustrated, angry or unhappy, never hold anyone except ourselves – that is, our judgements – accountable. An ignorant person is inclined to blame others for his own misfortune. To blame oneself is proof of progress. But the wise man never has to blame another *or* himself.

CHAPTER 6

Don't pride yourself on any assets but your own. We could put up with a horse if it bragged of its beauty. But don't you see that when *you* boast of having a beautiful horse, you are taking credit for the horse's traits? What quality belongs to you? The intelligent use of impressions. If you use impressions as nature prescribes, go ahead and indulge your pride, because then you will be celebrating a quality distinctly your own.

CHAPTER 7

If you are a sailor on board a ship that makes port, you may decide to go ashore to bring back water. Along the way you may stop to collect shellfish, or pick greens. But you always have to remember the ship and listen for the captain's signal to return. When he calls, you have to drop everything, otherwise you could be bound and thrown on board like the livestock.

So it is in life. If, instead of greens and shellfish, you have taken on a wife and child, so much the better. But when the captain calls, you must be prepared to leave them behind, and not give them another thought. If you are advanced in years, don't wander too far, or you won't make it back in time when the summons reaches you.

CHAPTER 8

Don't hope that events will turn out the way you want, welcome events in whichever way they happen: this is the path to peace.

CHAPTER 9

Sickness is a problem for the body, not the mind – unless the mind decides that it is a problem. Lameness, too, is the body's problem, not the mind's. Say this to yourself whatever the circumstance and you will find without fail that the problem pertains to something else, not to you.

CHAPTER 10

For every challenge, remember the resources you have within you to cope with it. Provoked by the sight of a handsome man or a beautiful woman, you will discover within you the contrary power of self-restraint. Faced with pain, you will discover the power of endurance. If you are insulted, you will discover patience. In time, you will grow to be confident that there is not a single impression that you will not have the moral means to tolerate.

CHAPTER 11

Under no circumstances ever say 'I have lost something,' only 'I returned it.' Did a child of yours die? No, it was returned. Your wife died? No, *she* was returned. 'My land was confiscated.' No, it too was returned.

'But the person who took it was a thief.'

Why concern yourself with the means by which the original giver effects its return? As long as he entrusts it to you, look after it as something yours to enjoy only for a time – the way a traveller regards a hotel.

CHAPTER 12

[1] If you want to make progress, drop reflections like: 'I will end up destitute if I don't take better care of my affairs,' or, 'Unless I discipline my slave, he'll wind up good for nothing.' It is better to die of hunger free of

grief and apprehension than to live affluent and uneasy. Better that your slave should be bad than that you should be unhappy.

[2] For that reason, starting with things of little value – a bit of spilled oil, a little stolen wine – repeat to yourself: 'For such a small price I buy tranquillity and peace of mind.' But nothing is completely free. So when you call your slave, be prepared for the possibility that he might ignore you, or if he does answer, that he won't do what he's told. He is not worth entrusting with your peace of mind.

CHAPTER 13

If you want to make progress, put up with being perceived as ignorant or naive in worldly matters, don't aspire to a reputation for sagacity. If you do impress others as somebody, don't altogether believe it. You have to realize, it isn't easy to keep your will in agreement with nature, as well as externals. Caring about the one inevitably means you are going to shortchange the other.

CHAPTER 14

[1] You are a fool to want your children, wife or friends to be immortal; it calls for powers beyond you, and gifts not yours to either own or give. It is equally naive to ask that your slave be honest; it amounts to asking that vice be not vice but something different. You can, however, avoid meeting with disappointment in your desires; focus on

this, then, since it is in the scope of your capacities. [2] We are at the mercy of whoever wields authority over the things we either desire or detest. If you would be free, then, do not wish to have, or avoid, things that other people control, because then you must serve as their slave.

CHAPTER 15

Remember to act always as if you were at a symposium. When the food or drink comes around, reach out and take some politely; if it passes you by don't try pulling it back. And if it has not reached you yet, don't let your desire run ahead of you, be patient until your turn comes. Adopt a similar attitude with regard to children, wife, wealth and status, and in time, you will be entitled to dine with the gods. Go further and decline these goods even when they are on offer and you will have a share in the gods' power as well as their company. That is how Diogenes, Heraclitus and philosophers like them came to be called, and considered, divine.

CHAPTER 16

Whenever you see someone in tears, distraught because they are parted from a child, or have met with some material loss, be careful lest the impression move you to believe that their circumstances are truly bad. Have ready the reflection that they are not upset by what happened – because other people are not upset when the same thing happens to them – but by their own view of the matter. Nevertheless, you should not disdain to sympathize with them, at least with comforting words, or even to the extent of sharing outwardly in their grief. But do not commiserate with your whole heart and soul.

CHAPTER 17

Remember that you are an actor in a play, the nature of which is up to the director to decide. If he wants the play to be short, it will be short, if he wants it long, it will be long. And if he casts you as one of the poor, or as a cripple, as a king or as a commoner – whatever role is assigned, the accomplished actor will accept and perform it with impartial skill. But the assignment of roles belongs to another.

CHAPTER 18

If you hear a raven croak inauspiciously, do not be alarmed by the impression. Make a mental distinction at once, and say, 'These omens hold no significance for me; they only pertain to my body, property, family, or reputation. For *me* every sign is auspicious, if I want it to be, because, whatever happens, I can derive some benefit from it.'

CHAPTER 19

[1] You will never have to experience defeat if you avoid contests whose outcome is outside your control. [2]

Don't let outward appearances mislead you into thinking that someone with more prestige, power or some other distinction must on that account be happy. If the essence of the good lies within us, then there is no place for jealousy or envy, and you will not care about being a general, a senator or a consul – only about being free. And the way to be free is to look down on externals.

CHAPTER 20

Remember, it is not enough to be hit or insulted to be harmed, you must, believe that you are being harmed. If someone succeeds in provoking you, realize that your mind is complicit in the provocation. Which is why it is essential that we not respond impulsively to impressions; take a moment before reacting, and you will find it is easier to maintain control.

CHAPTER 21

Keep the prospect of death, exile and all such apparent tragedies before you every day – especially death – and you will never have an abject thought, or desire anything to excess.

CHAPTER 22

If you commit to philosophy, be prepared at once to be laughed at and made the butt of many snide remarks, like, 'Suddenly there's a philosopher among us!' and 'What makes him so pretentious now?' Only *don't* be pretentious: just stick to your principles as if God had made you accept the role of philosopher. And rest assured that, if you remain true to them, the same people who made fun of you will come to admire you in time; whereas, if you let these people dissuade you from your choice, you will earn their derision twice over.

CHAPTER 23

If you are ever tempted to look for outside approval, realize that you have compromised your integrity. So be satisfied just being a philosopher, and if you need a witness in addition, be your own; and you will be all the witness you could desire.

CHAPTER 24

[1] Don't let thoughts like the following disturb you: 'I am going to live a life of no distinction, a nobody in complete obscurity.' Is lack of distinction bad? Because if it is, other people cannot be the cause of it, any more than they can be the cause of another's disgrace. Is it solely at your discretion that you are elevated to office, or invited to a party? No; so it cannot be a dishonour if you are not. And how can you be 'a nobody in obscurity' when you only have to be somebody in the areas you

control – the areas, that is, where you have the ability to shine?

[2] But your friends, you say, will be helpless. If by 'helpless' you mean that they won't get money from you, and you won't be able to make them Roman citizens – well, whoever told you that responsibility for such things belongs to us? Besides, who can give another what he does not have himself? 'Make money,' someone says, 'so that we can all share in it.' [3] If I can make money while remaining honest, trustworthy and dignified, show me how and I will do it. But if you expect me to sacrifice my own values, just so you can get your hands on things that aren't even good – well, you can see yourself how thoughtless and unfair you're being. Which would you rather have, anyway – money, or a worthy and faithful friend? So why not support me to that end, rather than asking me to engage in behaviour that involves the loss of these qualities?

[4] 'But my community will be helpless – to the extent that I can help.' Again, what kind of help do you have in mind? You can't give it buildings or baths, true, but so what? The blacksmith can't give it shoes, nor can the cobbler supply it with arms. It's enough if everyone plays their respective part. I mean, wouldn't you benefit your community by adding another lawful and loyal citizen to its rolls?

'Yes.'

Then evidently you have it in you to benefit it all on your own.

'Well, what will my profession in the community be?'

Whatever position you are equipped to fill, so long as you preserve the man of trust and integrity. [5] If you lose that in your zeal to be a public benefactor, what use in the end will you be to the community once you have been rendered shameless and corrupt?

CHAPTER 25

[1] Someone was preferred above you at a formal dinner or awards banquet, and their advice was solicited before yours. If such marks of esteem are good, you should be pleased for the other person; if they are not, don't chafe because you did not get them. And remember, if you do not engage in the same acts as others with a view to gaining such honours, you cannot expect the same results. [2] A person who will not stoop to flattery does not get to have the flatterer's advantages. One who dances attendance on a superior is rewarded differently from someone who sits out. Refuse to praise someone and you cannot expect the same compensation as a flatterer. It would be unfair and greedy on your part, then, to decline to pay the price that these privileges entail and hope to get them free.

[3] How much is a head of lettuce worth? One obol, perhaps? Now if someone pays an obol and gets the head of lettuce, while you will not pay this much and therefore go without, don't imagine that you necessarily come off second best. As he has the lettuce, you still have the money. [4] And it's much the same in our case. You were not invited to someone's party, because you

wouldn't pay the host the price of admission, namely paying her court and singing her praises. So pay the bill, if you expect to gain by it, and give no further thought to the expense. But if you won't pay the bill and still want the benefits, you are not only greedy but a fool. [5] If you forgo the meal, however, must it mean that you leave empty-handed? You have the advantage of not having to praise the host, which you find disagreeable (and won't have to put up with the insolence of his slaves).

CHAPTER 26

We can familiarize ourselves with the will of nature by calling to mind our common experiences. When a friend breaks a glass, we are quick to say, 'Oh, bad luck.' It's only reasonable, then, that when a glass of your own breaks, you accept it in the same patient spirit. Moving on to graver things: when somebody's wife or child dies, to a man we all routinely say, 'Well, that's part of life.' But if one of our own family is involved, then right away it's 'Poor, poor me!' We would do better to remember how we react when a similar loss afflicts others.

CHAPTER 27

Just as a target is not set up in order to be missed, so evil is no natural part of the world's design.

CHAPTER 28

If your body was turned over to just anyone, you would doubtless take exception. Why aren't you ashamed that you have made your mind vulnerable to anyone who happens to criticize you, so that it automatically becomes confused and upset?

CHAPTER 29

[1] Reflect on what every project entails in both its initial and subsequent stages before taking it up. Otherwise you will likely tackle it enthusiastically at first, since you haven't given thought to what comes next; but when things get difficult you'll wind up quitting the project in disgrace. [2] You want to win at the Olympics? So do I – who doesn't? It's a glorious achievement; but reflect on what's entailed both now and later on before committing to it. You have to submit to discipline, maintain a strict diet, abstain from rich foods, exercise under compulsion at set times in weather hot and cold, refrain from drinking water or wine whenever you want – in short, you have to hand yourself over to your trainer as if he were your doctor. And then there are digging contests to endure, and times when you will dislocate your wrist, turn your ankle, swallow quantities of sand, be whipped – and end up losing all the same.

[3] Consider all this, and if you still want to, then give athletics a go. If you don't pause to think, though, you'll

end up doing what children do, playing at wrestler one minute, then gladiator, then actor, then musician. And you – you're an athlete now, next a gladiator, an orator, a philosopher – but nothing with all your heart. You're like a monkey who imitates whatever it happens to see, infatuated with one thing after another. You haven't approached anything attentively, or thought things through; your approach to projects is casual and capricious.

[4] Some people, likewise, see a philosopher or hear someone like Euphrates lecture (only, who can lecture like him?) and get it in their heads to become philosophers too. [5] Listen, friend, research the role, then assess your capacity to fill it, just as you assess your arms, thighs and back if you hope to be a wrestler or pentathlete. [6] We are not all cut out for the same thing. Do you think that as a philosopher you can eat and drink, or exercise desire and aversion, as you do at present? You have to stay up nights, put up with pain, leave your family, be looked down on by slaves, suffer ridicule from strangers, be outdone in status, in power, in legal matters – get the worst of it, in other words, down to the last little thing. [7] Ponder whether you're prepared to pay this price for serenity, freedom and calm. If not, then don't go near it – don't, like children, be a philosopher now, a tax officer later, then an orator or politician. These roles don't mix; you have to be one person, good or bad. You have to care either for your mind or for material things; specialize in what is within you or without – which is to say, you have to stick to the role of philosopher or layman.

CHAPTER 30

Duties are broadly defined by social roles. This man is your father: the relationship demands from you support, constant deference and tolerance for his verbal, even his physical, abuse.

'But he's a bad father.'

Look, nature has endeared you to a father, not necessarily a *good* one.

'My brother is unfair to me.'

Well then, keep up your side of the relationship; don't concern yourself with his behaviour, only with what *you* must do to keep your will in tune with nature. Another person will not hurt you without your cooperation; you are hurt the moment you believe yourself to be.

The titles of neighbour, citizen and general will likewise suggest to you what functions they entail, once you begin to give social relationships their due in your daily deliberations.

CHAPTER 31

[1] Realize that the chief duty we owe the gods is to hold the correct beliefs about them: that they exist, that they govern the world justly and well, and that they have put you here for one purpose – to obey them and welcome whatever happens, in the conviction that it is a product of the highest intelligence. This way you won't ever blame the gods or charge them with neglect. [2] And this

cannot happen unless you stop applying 'good' and 'bad' to externals and only describe things under our control that way. Because, if you regard any external as good or bad, and fail to get what you want or get what you don't want instead, you will blame the gods and inevitably hate them for being the cause of your trouble.

[3] Every living thing by nature shrinks and turns away from whatever it considers harmful or malicious, just as it loves and gravitates toward what is helpful and sympathetic. Anyone who imagines that they are being wronged can no more love the offender than the offence. [4] And so we find even fathers being blamed by their children, when they fail to give them what the child regards as good. It is the same reason Polyneices and Eteocles became enemies – the idea each had that it would be better to rule alone. It is why farmers curse the gods; why sailors, traders and men who have lost wives or children curse them too. Piety cannot exist apart from self-interest. The upshot is, when you practise using desire and aversion correctly, you practise being pious.

[5] At the same time, it is never wrong to make sacrifice, pour libations, or offer first fruits in the traditional manner, as long as it is done attentively and not carelessly or by rote, and you neither offer too little nor spend beyond your means.

CHAPTER 32

[1] In your approach to divination, bear in mind that you don't know what will happen, you go in order to learn it

from the prophet. A philosopher, however, arrives already knowing the value of what's to come. If it's anything outside his sphere of influence, he knows it can be neither good nor bad. [2] So if you consult a prophet, leave desire, fear, and aversion behind, in the assurance that the future, *per se*, is indifferent, and nothing to you. You can make use of it, whatever it is, and there's not a soul who can stop you. Approach the gods with a dignified attitude, think of them as your advisers. But once their advice has been given, remember the source and consider who you would be slighting if you were to set that advice aside.

[3] Make use of divination the way Socrates thought it should be used, i.e. solely when it's a matter of learning the future – not when there's a problem that can be resolved by the application of reason (another human resource). Don't, for example, resort to divination if you are dutybound to come to the defence of your country or share in some danger threatening a friend. Suppose the seer declares the omens unfavourable – which, in cases like this, could spell exile for you, physical injury, even death. And still reason demands that you stick by your friend, or help defend your country. On that score we have only to consult the greatest prophet of all, Apollo: he refused to let someone enter his temple who had once ignored cries for help from a friend under assault from robbers.

CHAPTER 33

[1] Settle on the type of person you want to be and stick to it, whether alone or in company.

[2] Let silence be your goal for the most part; say only what is necessary, and be brief about it. On the rare occasions when you're called upon to speak, then speak, but never about banalities like gladiators, horses, sports, food and drink – commonplace stuff. Above all don't gossip about people, praising, blaming or comparing them. [3] Try to influence your friends to speak appropriately by your example. If you find yourself in unfamiliar company, however, keep quiet.

[4] Keep laughter to a minimum; do not laugh too often or too loud.

[5] If possible, refuse altogether to take an oath; resist, in any case, as far as circumstances will permit.

[6] Avoid fraternizing with non-philosophers. If you must, though, be careful not to sink to their level; because, you know, if a companion is dirty, his friends cannot help but get a little dirty too, no matter how clean they started out.

[7] Where the body is concerned, take only what is strictly necessary in the way of food, drink, clothing, shelter and household slaves. Cut out luxury and ostentation altogether.

[8] Concerning sex, stay as chaste as you can before marriage. If you do indulge, engage only in licit liaisons. Don't be harsh or judgemental towards others who have sex; if you are celibate yourself, don't advertise the fact.

[9] If you learn that someone is speaking ill of you, don't try to defend yourself against the rumours; respond instead with, 'Yes, and he doesn't know the half of it, because he could have said more.'

[10] There is no call to be a regular at the public games. But if the occasion should arise and you go, don't be seen siding with anyone except yourself; which is to say, hope only for what happens to happen, and for the actual winner to win; then you won't be unhappy. Yelling, jeering and excessive agitation should be avoided completely. Don't talk much about the event afterwards, or any more than is necessary to get it out of your system. Otherwise it becomes obvious that the experience captivated you.

[11] Don't too soon, or too lightly, attend other people's lectures; when you do go remain serious and reserved, without being disagreeable.

[12] When you are going to meet someone, especially someone deemed important, imagine to yourself what Socrates or Zeno would have done in the situation and you won't fail to get on, whatever happens. [13] When you are going to the house of someone influential, tell yourself that you won't find them in, that you will be locked out, that the door will be slammed in your face, that they won't give you the time of day. And, despite that, if it's the right thing to go, then go and face the consequences. Don't say to yourself later, 'It wasn't worth it.' That's the mark of a conventional person at odds with life.

[14] In your conversation, don't dwell at excessive length on your own deeds or adventures. Just because you enjoy recounting your exploits doesn't mean that others derive the same pleasure from hearing about them.

[15] And avoid trying to be funny. That way vulgarity

lies, and at the same time it's likely to lower you in your friends' estimation.

[16] It is also not a good idea to venture on profanity. If it happens, and you aren't out of line, you may even criticize a person who indulges in it. Otherwise, signal your dislike of his language by falling silent, showing unease or giving him a sharp look.

CHAPTER 34

As with impressions generally, if you get an impression of something pleasurable, watch yourself so that you are not carried away by it. Take a minute and let the matter wait on you. Then reflect on both intervals of time: the time you will have to experience the pleasure, and the time after its enjoyment that you will beat yourself up over it. Contrast that with how happy and pleased you'll be if you abstain. If the chance to do the deed presents itself, take extra care that you are not overcome by its seductiveness, pleasure and allure. Counter temptation by remembering how much better will be the knowledge that you resisted.

CHAPTER 35

If you decide to do something, don't shrink from being seen doing it, even if the majority of people disapprove. If you're wrong to do it, then you should shrink from doing it altogether; but if you're right, then why worry how people will judge you?

CHAPTER 36

Just as the propositions 'It is day' and 'It is night' together contribute much to disjunctive propositions, but nothing to conjunctive ones so, even allowing that taking the largest portion of a dish contributes to the health of the body, it contributes nothing to the communal spirit that a dinner party should typify. So when you dine in company, remember not only to consider what the food on offer can do for your health, have some consideration for your host's good health too.

CHAPTER 37

If you undertake a role beyond your means, you will not only embarrass yourself in that, you miss the chance of a role that you might have filled successfully.

CHAPTER 38

As you are careful when you walk not to step on a nail or turn your ankle, so you should take care not to do any injury to your character at the same time. Exercise such caution whenever we act, and we will perform the act with less risk of injury.

CHAPTER 39

Each man's body defines the limit of his material needs, as, on a small scale, the foot does with regard to shoes. Observe this principle, and you will never be in any confusion as to what those limits are. Exceed them, and you inevitably fall off a virtual cliff. As with shoes – if you don't limit yourself to what the foot needs, you wind up with gold heels, purple pumps or even embroidered slippers. There's no end once the natural limit has been exceeded.

CHAPTER 40

At the age of fourteen girls begin to be addressed by men as 'ladies'. From this they infer that the world honours them for nothing so much as their potential as sexual partners. Consequently, they become preoccupied with their appearance to the exclusion of everything else. They must be made to realize that they are entitled to be called 'ladies' only insofar as they cultivate modesty and self-respect.

CHAPTER 41

It shows a lack of refinement to spend a lot of time exercising, eating, drinking, defecating or copulating. Tending to the body's needs should be done incidentally, as it were; the mind and its functions require the bulk of our attention.

CHAPTER 42

Whenever anyone criticizes or wrongs you, remember that they are only doing or saying what they think is right. They cannot be guided by your views, only their own; so if their views are wrong, they are the ones who suffer insofar as they are misguided. I mean, if someone declares a true conjunctive proposition to be false, the proposition is unaffected, it is they who come off worse for having their ignorance exposed. With this in mind you will treat your critic with more compassion. Say to yourself each time, 'He did what he believed was right.'

CHAPTER 43

Every circumstance comes with two handles, with one of which you can hold it, while with the other conditions are insupportable. If your brother mistreats you, don't try to come to grips with it by dwelling on the wrong he's done (because that approach makes it unbearable); remind yourself that he's your brother, that you two grew up together; then you'll find that you can bear it.

CHAPTER 44

The following are non-sequiturs: 'I am richer, therefore superior to you'; or 'I am a better speaker, therefore a better person, than you.' These statements, on the other hand, are cogent: 'I am richer than you, therefore my wealth is superior to yours'; and 'I am a better speaker, therefore my diction is better than yours.' But *you* are neither wealth nor diction.

CHAPTER 45

Someone bathes in haste; don't say he bathes badly, but in haste. Someone drinks a lot of wine; don't say he drinks badly, but a lot. Until you know their reasons, how do you know that their actions are vicious? This will save you from perceiving one thing clearly, but then assenting to something different.

CHAPTER 46

[1] Never identify yourself as a philosopher or speak much to non-philosophers about your principles; act in line with those principles. At a dinner party, for instance, don't tell people the right way to eat, just eat the right way. Remember how Socrates so effaced himself that people used to approach him seeking an introduction to philosophers, and he would graciously escort them; that's how careless he was of the slight. [2] If conversation turns to a philosophical topic, keep silent for the most part, since you run the risk of spewing forth a lot of ill-digested information. If your silence is taken for ignorance, but it doesn't upset you – well, that's the real sign that you have begun to be a philosopher. Sheep don't bring their owners grass to prove to them how much they've eaten, they digest it inwardly and

outwardly bring forth milk and wool. So don't make a
show of your philosophical learning to the uninitiated,
show them by your actions what you have absorbed.

CHAPTER 47

When your body gets used to simple living, don't preen
over it; if you're a water drinker, don't take every opportunity to announce it. If you want to train for physical
austerities, do it for yourself, not for outsiders. Don't
embrace marble statues; but if you happen to be very
thirsty, try taking some cold water in your mouth and
spitting it out – and don't tell anyone.

CHAPTER 48

[1] The mark and attitude of the ordinary man: never
look for help or harm from yourself, only from outsiders. The mark and attitude of the philosopher: look for
help and harm exclusively from yourself.

[2] And the signs of a person making progress: he
never criticizes, praises, blames or points the finger, or
represents himself as knowing or amounting to anything. If he experiences frustration or disappointment,
he points the finger at himself. If he's praised, he's more
amused than elated. And if he's criticized, he won't
bother to respond. He walks around as if he were an
invalid, careful not to move a healing limb before it's at
full strength. [3] He has expunged all desire, and made
the things that are contrary to nature and in his control

the sole target of his aversion. Impulse he only uses with detachment. He does not care if he comes across as stupid or naive. In a word, he keeps an eye on himself as if he were his own enemy lying in ambush.

CHAPTER 49

Whenever someone prides himself on being able to understand and comment on Chrysippus' books, think to yourself, 'If Chrysippus had written more clearly, this person would have nothing to be proud of.' As for me, I care only about understanding nature, and following its leads. So I look for someone to interpret nature for me, and after hearing that Chrysippus can, I turn to him. So far, I have no cause for conceit. When I find that Chrysippus really can interpret nature, it still remains for me to act on his suggestions – which is the only thing one can be proud of. If I admire the interpretation, I have turned into a literary critic instead of a philosopher, the only difference being that, instead of Homer, I'm interpreting Chrysippus. But whenever people ask me to interpret Chrysippus for them, I only feel shame that my actions don't meet or measure up to what he says.

CHAPTER 50

Whatever your mission, stick by it as if it were a law and you would be committing sacrilege to betray it. Pay no attention to whatever people might say; this no longer should influence you.

CHAPTER 51

[1] How long will you wait before you demand the best of yourself, and trust reason to determine what is best? You have been introduced to the essential doctrines, and claim to understand them. So what kind of teacher are you waiting for that you delay putting these principles into practice until he comes? You're a grown man already, not a child any more. If you remain careless and lazy, making excuse after excuse, fixing one day after another when you will finally take yourself in hand, your lack of progress will go unnoticed, and in the end you will have lived and died unenlightened.

[2] Finally decide that you are an adult who is going to devote the rest of your life to making progress. Abide by what seems best as if it were an inviolable law. When faced with anything painful or pleasurable, anything bringing glory or disrepute, realize that the crisis is now, that the Olympics have started, and waiting is no longer an option; that the chance for progress, to keep or lose, turns on the events of a single day. [3] That's how Socrates got to be the person he was, by depending on reason to meet his every challenge. You're not yet Socrates, but you can still live as if you want to be him.

CHAPTER 52

[1] The first and most important field of philosophy is the application of principles such as 'Do not lie.' Next

come the proofs, such as why we should not lie. The third field supports and articulates the proofs, by asking, for example, 'How does this prove it? What exactly is a proof, what is logical inference, what is contradiction, what is truth, what is falsehood?' [2] Thus, the third field is necessary because of the second, and the second because of the first. The most important, though, the one that should occupy most of our time, is the first. But we do just the opposite. We are preoccupied with the third field and give that all our attention, passing the first by altogether. The result is that we lie – but have no difficulty proving why we shouldn't.

CHAPTER 53

[1] In every circumstance we should have the following sentiments handy:
Lead me, Zeus, lead me, Destiny,
To the goal I was long ago assigned
And I will follow without hesitation. Even should I resist,
In a spirit of perversity, I will have to follow nonetheless.
[2] *Whoever yields to necessity graciously*
We account wise in God's ways.
[3] 'Dear Crito if it pleases the gods, so be it.'
[4] 'Anytus and Meletus can kill me, but they cannot harm me.'

On the Shortness of Life

Most human beings, Paulinus, complain about the meanness of nature, because we are born for a brief span of life, and because this spell of time that has been given to us rushes by so swiftly and rapidly that with very few exceptions life ceases for the rest of us just when we are getting ready for it. Nor is it just the man in the street and the unthinking mass of people who groan over this – as they see it – universal evil: the same feeling lies behind complaints from even distinguished men. Hence the dictum of the greatest of doctors: 'Life is short, art is long.' Hence too the grievance, most improper to a wise man, which Aristotle expressed when he was taking nature to task for indulging animals with such long existences that they can live through five or ten human lifetimes, while a far shorter limit is set for men who are born to a great and extensive destiny. It is not that we have a short time to live, but that we waste a lot of it. Life is long enough, and a sufficiently generous amount has been given to us for the highest achievements if it were all well invested. But when it is wasted in heedless luxury and spent on no good activity, we are forced at last by death's final constraint to realize that it has passed away before we knew it was passing. So it is: we are not given a short life but we make it short, and we are not ill-supplied but wasteful of it. Just as when ample and princely wealth falls to a bad owner it is squandered in a moment, but wealth however modest, if entrusted to a good custodian, increases with use, so our lifetime extends amply if you manage it properly.

Why do we complain about nature? She has acted kindly: life is long if you know how to use it. But one man is gripped by insatiable greed, another by a laborious dedication to useless tasks. One man is soaked in wine, another sluggish with idleness. One man is worn out by political ambition, which is always at the mercy of the judgement of others. Another through hope of profit is driven headlong over all lands and seas by the greed of trading. Some are tormented by a passion for army life, always intent on inflicting dangers on others or anxious about danger to themselves. Some are worn out by the self-imposed servitude of thankless attendance on the great. Many are occupied by either pursuing other people's money or complaining about their own. Many pursue no fixed goal, but are tossed about in ever-changing designs by a fickleness which is shifting, inconstant and never satisfied with itself. Some have no aims at all for their life's course, but death takes them unawares as they yawn languidly – so much so that I cannot doubt the truth of that oracular remark of the greatest of poets: 'It is a small part of life we really live.'

Indeed, all the rest is not life but merely time. Vices surround and assail men from every side, and do not allow them to rise again and lift their eyes to discern the truth, but keep them overwhelmed and rooted in their desires. Never can they recover their true selves. If by chance they achieve some tranquillity, just as a swell remains on the deep sea even after the wind has dropped, so they go on tossing about and never find rest from their desires. Do you think I am speaking only of those whose wickedness is acknowledged? Look at those whose good fortune people gather to see: they are choked by their own blessings. How many find their riches a burden! How many burst a blood vessel by their eloquence and their daily striving to show off their talents! How many are pale from constant pleasures! How many are left no freedom by the crowd of clients surrounding them! In a word, run through them all, from lowest to highest: one calls for legal assistance, another comes to help; one is on trial, another defends him, another gives a judgment; no one makes his claim to himself, but each is exploited for another's sake. Ask about those whose names are learned by heart, and you will see that they have these distinguishing marks: X cultivates Y and Y cultivates Z – no one bothers about himself. Again, certain people reveal the most stupid indignation: they complain about the pride of their superiors because they did not have time to give them an audience when they wanted one. But can anyone dare to complain about another's pride when he himself never has time for himself? Yet whoever you are, the great man has sometimes gazed upon you, even if his look was patronizing, he has bent his ears to your words, he has let you walk beside him. But you never deign to look at yourself or listen to yourself. So you have no reason to claim credit from anyone for those attentions, since you showed them not because you wanted someone else's company but because you could not bear your own.

Even if all the bright intellects who ever lived were to agree to ponder this one theme, they would never sufficiently express their surprise at this fog in the human mind. Men do not let anyone seize their estates, and if there is the slightest dispute about their boundaries they rush to stones and arms; but they allow others to encroach on their lives – why, they themselves even invite in those who will take over their lives. You will find no one willing to share out his money; but to how many does each of us divide up his life! People are frugal in guarding their personal property; but as soon as it comes to squandering time they are most wasteful of the one thing in which it is right to be stingy. So, I would like to fasten on someone from the older generation and say to him: 'I see that you have come to the last stage of human life; you are close upon your hundredth year, or even beyond: come now, hold an audit of your life. Reckon how much of your time has been taken up by a moneylender, how much by a mistress, a patron, a client, quarrelling with your wife, punishing your slaves, dashing about the city on your social obligations. Consider also the diseases which we have brought on ourselves, and the time too which has been unused. You will find that you have fewer years than you reckon. Call to mind when you ever had a fixed purpose; how few days have passed as you had planned; when you were ever at your own disposal; when your face wore its natural expression; when your mind was undisturbed; what work you have achieved in such a long life; how many have plundered your life when you were unaware of your losses; how much you have lost through groundless sorrow, foolish joy, greedy desire, the seductions of society; how little of your own was left to you. You will realize that you are dying prematurely.'

So what is the reason for this? You are living as if destined to live for ever; your own frailty never occurs to you; you don't notice how much time has already passed, but squander it as though you had a full and overflowing supply – though all the while that very day which you are devoting to somebody or something may be your last. You act like mortals in all that you fear, and like immortals in all that you desire. You will hear many people saying: 'When I am fifty I shall retire into leisure; when I am sixty I shall give up public duties.' And what guarantee do you have of a longer life? Who will allow your course to proceed as you arrange it? Aren't you ashamed to keep for yourself just the remnants of your life, and to devote to wisdom only that time which cannot be spent on any business? How late it is to begin really to live just when life must end! How stupid to forget our mortality, and put off sensible plans to our fiftieth and sixtieth years, aiming to begin life from a point at which few have arrived!

You will notice that the most powerful and highly stationed men let drop remarks in which they pray for leisure, praise it, and rate it higher than all their blessings. At times they long to descend from their pinnacles if they can in safety; for even if nothing external assails or agitates it, high fortune of itself comes crashing down.

The deified Augustus, to whom the gods granted more than to anyone else, never ceased to pray for rest and to seek a respite from public affairs. Everything he said always reverted to this theme – his hope for leisure. He used to beguile his labours with this consolation, sweet though false, that one day he would live to please himself. In a letter he wrote to the senate, after he promised that his rest would not be lacking in dignity nor inconsistent with his former glory, I find these words: 'But it is more impressive to carry out these things than to promise them. Nevertheless, since the delightful reality is still a long way off, my longing for that much desired time has led me to anticipate some of its delight by the pleasure arising from words.' So valuable did leisure seem to him that because he could not enjoy it in actuality, he did so mentally in advance. He who saw that everything depended on himself alone, who decided the fortune of individuals and nations, was happiest when thinking of that day on which he would lay aside his own greatness. He knew from experience how much sweat those blessings gleaming through every land cost him, how many secret anxieties they concealed. He was forced to fight first with his fellow-countrymen, then with his colleagues, and finally with his relations, shedding blood on land and sea. Driven to fight in Macedonia, Sicily, Egypt, Syria, Asia – almost every country – he turned his armies against foreign enemies when they were tired of shedding Roman blood. While he was establishing peace in the Alps and subduing enemies established in the middle of his peaceful empire; while he was extending his boundaries beyond the Rhine, the Euphrates and the Danube, at Rome itself Murena, Caepio, Lepidus, Egnatius and others were sharpening their swords against him. Nor had he yet escaped their plots when his daughter and all the noble youths bound to her by adultery as though by an oath kept alarming his feeble old age, as did Iullus and a second formidable woman linked to an Antony. He cut away these ulcers, limbs and all, but others took their place: just like a body with a surfeit of blood which is always subject to a haemorrhage somewhere. So he longed for leisure, and as his hopes and thoughts dwelt on that he found relief for his labours: this was the prayer of the man who could grant the prayers of mankind.

When Marcus Cicero was cast among men like Catiline and Clodius and Pompey and Crassus—some of them undisguised enemies and some doubtful friends – when he was tossed about in the storm that struck the state, he tried to hold it steady as it went to its doom; but at last he was swept away. He had neither peace in prosperity nor patience in adversity, and how often does he curse that very consulship, which he had praised without ceasing though not without good reason! What woeful words he uses in a letter to Atticus when the elder Pompey had been conquered, and his son was still trying to revive his defeated forces in Spain! 'Do you want to know,' he said, 'what I am doing here? I am staying a semi-prisoner in my Tusculan villa.' He then goes on to bewail his former life, to complain of the present, and to despair of the future. Cicero called himself a semi-prisoner, but really and truly the wise man will never go so far as to use such an abject term. He will never be a semi-prisoner, but will always enjoy freedom which is solid and complete, at liberty to be his own master and higher than all others. For what can be above the man who is above fortune?

Livius Drusus, a bold and vigorous man, had proposed laws which renewed the evil policy of the Gracchi, and he was supported by a huge crowd from all over Italy. But he could see no successful outcome for his measures, which he could neither carry through nor abandon once embarked upon; and he is said to have cursed the turbulent life he had always lived, saying that he alone had never had a holiday even as a child. For while still a ward and dressed as a youth he ventured to speak to a jury in favour of some accused men, and to acquire influence in the law courts, with so much effect that, as we all know, he forced certain verdicts favourable to his clients. To what lengths would so precocious an ambition not go? You might have known that such premature boldness would result in terrible trouble, both public and private. So he was too late in complaining that he had never had a holiday, since from his boyhood he had been a serious troublemaker in the Forum. It is uncertain whether he died by his own hand, for he collapsed after receiving a sudden wound in the groin, some people doubting whether his death was self-inflicted, but no one doubting that it was timely.

It would be superfluous to mention any more who, though seeming to others the happiest of mortals, themselves bore true witness against themselves by their expressed hatred of every action of their lives. Yet they did not change themselves or anyone else by these complaints, for after their explosion of words their feelings reverted to normal.

Assuredly your lives, even if they last more than a thousand years, will shrink into the tiniest span: those vices will swallow up any space of time. The actual time you have – which reason can prolong though it naturally passes quickly – inevitably escapes you rapidly: for you do not grasp it or hold it back or try to delay that swiftest of all things, but you let it slip away as though it were something superfluous and replaceable.

But among the worst offenders I count those who spend all their time in drinking and lust, for these are the worst preoccupations of all. Other people, even if they are possessed by an illusory semblance of glory, suffer from a respectable delusion. You can give me a list of miserly men, or hot-tempered men who indulge in unjust hatreds or wars: but they are all sinning in a more manly way. It is those who are on a headlong course of gluttony and lust who are stained with dishonour. Examine how all these people spend their time – how long they devote to their accounts, to laying traps for others or fearing those laid for themselves, to paying court to others or being courted themselves, to giving or receiving bail, to banquets (which now count as official business): you will see how their activities, good or bad, do not give them even time to breathe.

Finally, it is generally agreed that no activity can be successfully pursued by an individual who is preoccupied – not rhetoric or liberal studies – since the mind when distracted absorbs nothing deeply, but rejects everything which is, so to speak, crammed into it. Living is the least important activity of the preoccupied man; yet there is nothing which is harder to learn. There are many instructors in the other arts to be found everywhere: indeed, some of these arts mere boys have grasped so thoroughly that they can even teach them. But learning how to live takes a whole life, and, which may surprise you more, it takes a whole life to learn how to die. So many of the finest men have put aside all their encumbrances, renouncing riches and business and pleasure, and made it their one aim up to the end of their lives to know how to live. Yet most of these have died confessing that they did not yet know – still less can those others know. Believe me, it is the sign of a great man, and one who is above human error, not to allow his time to be frittered away: he has the longest possible life simply because whatever time was available he devoted entirely to himself. None of it lay fallow and neglected, none of it under another's control; for being an extremely thrifty guardian of his time he never found anything for which it was worth exchanging. So he had enough time; but those into whose lives the public have made great inroads inevitably have too little.

Nor must you think that such people do not sometimes recognize their loss. Indeed, you will hear many of those to whom great prosperity is a burden sometimes crying out amidst their hordes of clients or their pleadings in law courts or their other honourable miseries. 'It's impossible to live.' Of course it's impossible. All those who call you to themselves draw you away from yourself. How many days has that defendant stolen from you? Or that candidate? Or that old lady worn out with burying her heirs? Or that man shamming an illness to excite the greed of legacy-hunters? Or that influential friend who keeps people like you not for friendship but for display? Mark off, I tell you, and review the days of your life: you will see that very few – the useless remnants – have been left to you. One man who has achieved the badge of office he coveted longs to lay it aside, and keeps repeating, 'Will this year never end?' Another man thought it a great coup to win the chance of giving games, but, having given them, he says, 'When shall I be rid of them?' That advocate is grabbed on every side throughout the Forum, and fills the whole place with a huge crowd extending further than he can be heard: but he says, 'When will vacation come?' Everyone hustles his life along, and is troubled by a longing for the future and weariness of the present. But the man who spends all his time on his own needs, who organizes every day as though it were his last, neither longs for nor fears the next day. For what new pleasures can any hour now bring him? He has tried everything, and enjoyed everything to repletion. For the rest, Fortune can dispose as she likes: his life is now secure. Nothing can be taken from this life, and you can only add to it as if giving to a man who is already full and satisfied food which he does not want but can hold. So you must not think a man has lived long because he has white hair and wrinkles: he has not lived long, just existed long. For suppose you should think that a man had had a long voyage who had been caught in a raging storm as he left harbour, and carried hither and thither and driven round and round in a circle by the rage of opposing winds? He did not have a long voyage, just a long tossing about.

I am always surprised to see some people demanding the time of others and meeting a most obliging response. Both sides have in view the reason for which the time is asked and neither regards the time itself – as if nothing there is being asked for and nothing given. They are trifling with life's most precious commodity, being deceived because it is an intangible thing, not open to inspection and therefore reckoned very cheap – in fact, almost without any value. People are delighted to accept pensions and gratuities, for which they hire out their labour or their support or their services. But nobody works out the value of time: men use it lavishly as if it cost nothing. But if death threatens these same people, you will see them praying to their doctors; if they are in fear of capital punishment, you will see them prepared to spend their all to stay alive. So inconsistent are they in their feelings. But if each of us could have the tally of his future years set before him, as we can of our past years, how alarmed. would be those who saw only a few years ahead, and how carefully would they use them! And yet it is easy to organize an amount, however small, which is assured; we have to be more careful in preserving what will cease at an unknown point.

But you are not to think that these people do not know how precious time is. They commonly say to those they are particularly fond of that they are ready to give them some of their years. And they do give them without being aware of it; but the gift is such that they themselves lose without adding anything to the others. But what they actually do not know is whether they are losing; thus they can bear the loss of what they do not know has gone. No one will bring back the years; no one will restore you to yourself. Life will follow the path it began to take, and will neither reverse nor check its course. It will cause no commotion to remind you of its swiftness, but glide on quietly. It will not lengthen itself for a king's command or a people's favour. As it started out on its first day, so it will run on, nowhere pausing or turning aside. What will be the outcome? You have been preoccupied while life hastens on. Meanwhile death will arrive, and you have no choice in making yourself available for that.

Can anything be more idiotic than certain people who boast of their foresight? They keep themselves officiously preoccupied in order to improve their lives; they spend their lives in organizing their lives. They direct their purposes with an eye to a distant future. But putting things off is the biggest waste of life: it snatches away each day as it comes, and denies us the present by promising the future. The greatest obstacle to living is expectancy, which hangs upon tomorrow and loses today. You are arranging what lies in Fortune's control, and abandoning what lies in yours. What are you looking at? To what goal are you straining? The whole future lies in uncertainty: live immediately. Listen to the cry of our greatest poet, who as though inspired with divine utterance sings salutary verses:

> Life's finest day for wretched mortals here
> Is always first to flee.

'Why do you linger?' he means. 'Why are you idle? If you don't grasp it first, it flees.' And even if you do grasp it, it will still flee. So you must match time's swiftness with your speed in using it, and you must drink quickly as though from a rapid stream that will not always flow. In chastising endless delay, too, the poet very elegantly speaks not of the 'finest age' but 'finest day'. However greedy you are, why are you so unconcerned and so sluggish (while time flies so fast), extending months and years in a long sequence ahead of you? The poet is telling you about the day – and about this very day that is escaping. So can it be doubted that for wretched

44

mortals – that is, the preoccupied – the finest day is always the first to flee? Old age overtakes them while they are still mentally childish, and they face it unprepared and unarmed. For they have made no provision for it, stumbling upon it suddenly and unawares, and without realizing that it was approaching day by day. Just as travellers are beguiled by conversation or reading or some profound meditation, and find they have arrived at their destination before they knew they were approaching it; so it is with this unceasing and extremely fast-moving journey of life, which waking or sleeping we make at the same pace – the preoccupied become aware of it only when it is over.

If I wanted to divide my theme into different headings and offer proofs, I would find many arguments to prove that the preoccupied find life very short. But Fabianus, who was not one of today's academic philosophers but the true old-fashioned sort, used to say that we must attack the passions by brute force and not by logic; that the enemy's line must be turned by a strong attack and not by pinpricks; for vices have to be crushed rather than picked at. Still, in order that the people concerned may be censured for their own individual faults, they must be taught and not just given up for lost.

Life is divided into three periods, past, present and future. Of these, the present is short, the future is doubtful, the past is certain. For this last is the one over which Fortune has lost her power, which cannot be brought back to anyone's control. But this is what preoccupied people lose: for they have no time to look back at their past, and even if they did, it is not pleasant to recall activities they are ashamed of. So they are unwilling to cast their minds back to times ill spent, which they dare not relive if their vices in recollection become obvious – even those vices whose insidious approach was disguised by the charm of some momentary pleasure. No one willingly reverts to the past unless all his actions have passed his own censorship, which is never deceived. The man who must fear his own memory is the one who has been ambitious in his greed, arrogant in his contempt, uncontrolled in his victories, treacherous in his deceptions, rapacious in his plundering, and wasteful in his squandering. And yet this is the period of our time which is sacred and dedicated, which has passed beyond all human risks and is removed from Fortune's sway, which cannot be harassed by want or fear or attacks of illness. It cannot be disturbed or snatched from us: it is an untroubled, everlasting possession. In the present we have only one day at a time, each offering a minute at a time. But all the days of the past will come to your call: you can detain and inspect them at your will – something which the preoccupied have no time to do. It is the mind which is tranquil and free from care which can roam through all the stages of its life: the minds of the preoccupied, as if harnessed in a yoke, cannot turn round and look behind them. So their lives vanish into an abyss; and just as it is no use pouring any amount of liquid into a container without a bottom to catch and hold it, so it does not matter how much time we are given if there is nowhere for it to settle; it escapes through the cracks and holes of the mind. The present time is extremely short, so much so that some people are unaware of it. For it is always on the move, flowing on in a rush; it ceases before it has come, and does not suffer delay any more than the firmament or the stars, whose unceasing movement never pauses in the same place. And so the preoccupied are concerned only with the present, and it is so short that it cannot be grasped, and even this is stolen from them while they are involved in their many distractions.

In a word, would you like to know how they do not live long? See how keen they are to live long. Feeble old men pray for a few more years; they pretend they are younger than they are; they comfort themselves by this deception and fool themselves as eagerly as if they fooled Fate at the same time. But when at last some illness has reminded them of their mortality, how terrified do they die, as if they were not just passing out of life but being dragged out of it. They exclaim that they were fools because they have not really lived, and that if only they can recover from this illness they will live in leisure. Then they reflect how pointlessly they acquired things they never would enjoy, and how all their toil has been in vain. But for those whose life is far removed from all business it must be amply long. None of it is frittered away, none of it scattered here and there, none of it committed to fortune, none of it lost through carelessness, none of it wasted on largesse, none of it superfluous: the whole of it, so to speak, is well invested. So, however short, it is fully sufficient, and therefore whenever his last day comes, the wise man will not hesitate to meet death with a firm step.

Perhaps you want to know whom I would call the preoccupied? You must not imagine I mean just those who are driven from the law court only by the arrival of the watchdogs; or those whom you see crushed either honourably in their own crowd of supporters or contemptuously in someone else's; or those whose social duties bring them forth from their own homes to dash them against someone else's doors; or those whom the praetor's auction spear occupies in acquiring disreputable gain which will one day turn rank upon them. Some men are preoccupied even in their leisure: in their country house, on their couch, in the midst of solitude, even when quite alone, they are their own worst company. You could not call theirs a life of leisure, but an idle preoccupation. Do you call that man leisured who arranges with anxious precision his Corinthian bronzes, the cost of which is inflated by the mania of a few collectors, and spends most of the day on rusty bits of metal? Who sits at a wrestling ring (for shame on us! We suffer from vices which are not even Roman), keenly following the bouts between boys? Who classifies his herds of pack-animals into pairs according to age and colour? Who pays for the maintenance of the latest athletes? Again, do you call those men leisured who spend many hours at the barber's simply to cut whatever grew overnight, to have a serious debate about every separate hair, to tidy up disarranged locks or to train thinning ones from the sides to lie over the forehead? How angry they get if the barber has been a bit careless – as if he were trimming a real man! How they flare up if any of their mane is wrongly cut off, if any of it is badly arranged, or if it doesn't all fall into the right ringlets! Which of them would not rather have his country ruffled than his hair? Which would not be more anxious about the elegance of his head than its safety? Which would not rather be trim than honourable? Do you call those men leisured who divide their time between the comb and the mirror? And what about those who busy themselves in composing, listening to, or learning songs, while they distort their voice, whose best and simplest tone nature intended to be the straight one, into the most unnatural modulations; who are always drumming with their fingers as they beat time to an imagined tune; whom you can hear humming to themselves even when they are summoned on a serious, often even sorrowful, affair? Theirs is not leisure but indolent occupation. And, good heavens, as for their banquets, I would not reckon on them as leisure times when I see how anxiously they arrange their silver, how carefully they gird up the tunics of their pageboys, how on tenterhooks they are to see how the cook has dealt with the boar, with what speed smooth-faced slaves rush around on their duties, with what skill birds are carved into appropriate portions, how carefully wretched little slaves wipe up the spittle of drunkards. By these means they cultivate a reputation for elegance and good taste, and to such an extent do their failings follow them into all areas of their private lives that they cannot eat or drink without ostentation.

I would also not count as leisured those who are carried around in a sedan chair and a litter, and turn up punctually for their drives as if it was forbidden to give them up; who have to be told when to bathe or to swim or to dine: they are so enervated by the excessive torpor of a self-indulgent mind that they cannot trust themselves to know if they are hungry. I am told that one of these self-indulgent people – if self-indulgence is the right word for unlearning the ordinary habits of human life – when he had been carried out from the bath and put in his sedan chair, asked, 'Am I now sitting down?' Do you think that this man, who doesn't know if he is sitting down, knows whether he is alive, whether he sees, whether he is at leisure? It is difficult to say whether I pity him more if he really did not know this or if he pretended not to know. They really experience forgetfulness of many things, but they also pretend to forget many things. They take delight in certain vices as proofs of their good fortune: it seems to be the lowly and contemptible man who knows what he is doing. After that see if you can accuse the mimes of inventing many details in order to attack luxury! In truth, they pass over more than they make up, and such a wealth of incredible vices have appeared in this generation, which shows talent in this one area, that we could now actually accuse the mimes of ignoring them. To think that there is anyone so lost in luxuries that he has to trust another to tell him if he is sitting down! So this one is not at leisure, and you must give him another description – he is ill, or even, he is dead: the man who is really at leisure is also aware of it. But this one who is only half alive, and needs to be told the positions of his own body – how can he have control over any of his time?

It would be tedious to mention individually those who have spent all their lives playing draughts or ball, or carefully cooking themselves in the sun. They are not at leisure whose pleasures involve a serious commitment. For example, nobody will dispute that those people are busy about nothing who spend their time on useless literary studies: even among the Romans there is now a large company of these. It used to be a Greek failing to want to know how many oarsmen Ulysses had, whether the *Iliad* or the *Odyssey* was written first, and whether too they were by the same author, and other questions of this kind, which if you keep them to yourself in no way enhance your private knowledge, and if you publish them make you appear more a bore than a scholar. But now the Romans too have been afflicted by the pointless enthusiasm for useless knowledge. Recently I heard somebody reporting which Roman general first did this or that: Duilius first won a naval battle; Curius Dentatus first included elephants in a triumph. So far these facts, even if they do not contribute to real glory, at least are concerned with exemplary services to the state: such knowledge will not do us any good, but it interests us because of the appeal of these pointless facts. We can also excuse those who investigate who first persuaded the Romans to

embark on a ship. That was Claudius, who for this reason was called Caudex because a structure linking
several wooden planks was called in antiquity a *caudex*.
Hence too the Law Tables are called *codices*, and even
today the boats which carry provisions up the Tiber are
called by the old-fashioned name *codicariae*. Doubtless
too it is of some importance to know that Valerius Cor-
vinus first conquered Messana, and was the first of the
family of the Valerii to be surnamed Messana from the
name of the captured city – the spelling of which was
gradually corrupted in everyday speech to Messalla.
Perhaps you will also allow someone to take seriously
the fact that Lucius Sulla first exhibited lions loose in
the Circus, though at other times they were shown in
fetters, and that javelin-throwers were sent by King
Bocchus to kill them. This too may be excused – but
does it serve any good purpose? – to know that Pompey
first exhibited in the Circus a fight involving eighteen
elephants, pitting innocent men against them in a
staged battle. A leader of the state and, as we are told,
a man of notable kindliness among the leaders of old,
he thought it would be a memorable spectacle to kill
human beings in a novel way. 'Are they to fight to the
death? Not good enough. Are they to be torn to pieces?
Not good enough. Let them be crushed by animals of
enormous bulk.' It would be better for such things to
be forgotten, lest in the future someone in power might
learn about them and not wish to be outdone in such a
piece of inhumanity. Oh, what darkness does great
prosperity cast over our minds! He thought himself

beyond nature's laws at the time that he was throwing so many crowds of wretched men to wild creatures from abroad, when he was setting such disparate creatures against each other, when he was shedding so much blood in front of the Roman people, who themselves were soon to be forced by him to shed their own blood. But later he himself, betrayed by Alexandrian treachery, offered himself to be stabbed by the lowest slave, only then realizing that his surname ('Great') was an empty boast.

But to return to the point from which I digressed, and to illustrate how some people spend useless efforts on these same topics, the man I referred to reported that Metellus in his triumph, after conquering the Carthaginians in Sicily, alone among all the Romans had 120 elephants led before his chariot, and that Sulla was the last of the Romans to have extended the *pomerium*, which it was the ancient practice to extend after acquiring Italian, but never provincial, territory. Is it better to know this than to know that the Aventine Hill, as he asserted, is outside the *pomerium* for one of two reasons, either because the plebs withdrew to it or because when Remus took the auspices there the birds had not been favourable – and countless further theories that are either false or very close to lies? For even if you admit that they say all this in good faith, even if they guarantee the truth of their statements, whose mistakes will thereby be lessened? Whose passions restrained? Who will be made more free, more just, more magnanimous? Our Fabianus used to say that sometimes he wondered whether it was better not to be involved in any researches than to get entangled in these.

Of all people only those are at leisure who make time for philosophy, only those are really alive. For they not only keep a good watch over their own lifetimes, but they annex every age to theirs. All the years that have passed before them are added to their own. Unless we are very ungrateful, all those distinguished founders of holy creeds were born for us and prepared for us a way of life. By the toil of others we are led into the presence of things which have been brought from darkness into light. We are excluded from no age, but we have access to them all; and if we are prepared in loftiness of mind to pass beyond the narrow confines of human weakness, there is a long period of time through which we can roam. We can argue with Socrates, express doubt with Carneades, cultivate retirement with Epicurus, overcome human nature with the Stoics, and exceed its limits with the Cynics. Since nature allows us to enter into a partnership with every age, why not turn from this brief and transient spell of time and give ourselves wholeheartedly to the past, which is limitless and eternal and can be shared with better men than we?

Those who rush about on social duties, disturbing both themselves and others, when they have duly finished their crazy round and have daily crossed everyone's threshold and passed by no open door, when they have carried around their self-interested greetings to houses that are miles apart, how few will they be able to see in a city so enormous and so distracted by varied desires? How many will there be who through sleepiness or self-indulgence or ungraciousness will exclude them? How many, after keeping them in an agony of waiting, will pretend to be in a hurry and rush past them? How many will avoid going out through a hall crowded with dependants, and escape through a secret door – as if it were not even more discourteous to deceive callers than to exclude them? How many, half asleep and sluggish after yesterday's drinking, will yawn insolently and have to be prompted a thousand times in a whisper before, scarcely moving their lips, they can greet by name the poor wretches who have broken their own slumbers in order to wait on another's?

You should rather suppose that those are involved in worthwhile duties who wish to have daily as their closest friends Zeno, Pythagoras, Democritus and all the other high priests of liberal studies, and Aristotle and Theophrastus. None of these will be too busy to see you, none of these will not send his visitor away happier and more devoted to himself, none of these will allow anyone to depart empty-handed. They are at home to all mortals by night and by day.

None of these will force you to die, but all will teach you how to die. None of them will exhaust your years, but each will contribute his years to yours. With none of these will conversation be dangerous, or his friendship fatal, or attendance on him expensive. From them you can take whatever you wish: it will not be their fault if you do not take your fill from them. What happiness, what a fine old age awaits the man who has made himself a client of these! He will have friends whose advice he can ask on the most important or the most trivial matters, whom he can consult daily about himself, who will tell him the truth without insulting him and praise him without flattery, who will offer him a pattern on which to model himself.

We are in the habit of saying that it was not in our power to choose the parents who were allotted to us, that they were given to us by chance. But we can choose whose children we would like to be. There are households of the noblest intellects: choose the one into which you wish to be adopted, and you will inherit not only their name but their property too. Nor will this property need to be guarded meanly or grudgingly: the more it is shared out, the greater it will become. These will offer you a path to immortality and raise you to a point from which no one is cast down. This is the only way to prolong mortality – even to convert it to immortality. Honours, monuments, whatever the ambitious have ordered by decrees or raised in public buildings are soon destroyed: there is nothing that the passage of time does not demolish and remove. But it cannot damage the works which philosophy has consecrated: no age will wipe them out, no age diminish them. The next and every following age will only increase the veneration for them, since envy operates on what is at hand, but we can more openly admire things from a distance. So the life of the philosopher extends widely: he is not confined by the same boundary as are others. He alone is free from the laws that limit the human race, and all ages serve him as though he were a god. Some time has passed: he grasps it in his recollection. Time is present: he uses it. Time is to come: he anticipates it. This combination of all times into one gives him a long life.

But life is very short and anxious for those who forget the past, neglect the present, and fear the future. When they come to the end of it, the poor wretches realize too late that for all this time they have been preoccupied in doing nothing. And the fact that they sometimes invoke death is no proof that their lives seem long. Their own folly afflicts them with restless emotions which hurl themselves upon the very things they fear: they often long for death because they fear it. Nor is this a proof that they are living for a long time that the day often seems long to them, or that they complain that the hours pass slowly until the time fixed for dinner arrives. For as soon as their preoccupations fail them, they are restless with nothing to do, not knowing how to dispose of their leisure or make the time pass. And so they are anxious for something else to do, and all the intervening time is wearisome: really, it is just as when a gladiatorial show has been announced, or they are looking forward to the appointed time of some other exhibition or amusement – they want to leap over the days in between. Any deferment of the longed-for event is tedious to them. Yet the time of the actual enjoyment is short and swift, and made much shorter through their own fault. For they dash from one pleasure to another and cannot stay steady in one desire. Their days are not long but odious: on the other hand, how short do the nights seem which they spend drinking or sleeping with harlots! Hence the lunacy of the poets, who encourage human frailty by their stories in which Jupiter, seduced by the pleasures of love-making, is seen to double the length of the night. What else is it but to inflame our vices when they quote the gods to endorse them, and as a precedent for our failings they offer – and excuse – the wantonness of the gods? Can the nights, which they purchase so dearly, not seem much too short to these people? They lose the day in waiting for the night, and the night in fearing the dawn.

Even their pleasures are uneasy and made anxious by various fears, and at the very height of their rejoicing the worrying thought steals over them: 'How long will this last?' This feeling has caused kings to bewail their power, and they were not so much delighted by the greatness of their fortune as terrified by the thought of its inevitable end. When that most arrogant king of Persia was deploying his army over vast plains, and could not number it but had to measure it, he wept because in a hundred years out of that huge army not a soul would be alive. But he who was weeping was the very man who would bring their fate upon them, and would destroy some on the sea, some on land, some in battle, some in flight, and in a very short time would wipe out all those for whose hundredth year he was afraid.

And what of the fact that even their joys are uneasy? The reason is that they are not based on firm causes, but they are agitated as groundlessly as they arise. But what kind of times can those be, do you think, which they themselves admit are wretched, since even the joys by which they are exalted and raised above humanity are pretty corrupt? All the greatest blessings create anxiety, and Fortune is never less to be trusted than when it is fairest. To preserve prosperity we need other prosperity, and to support the prayers which have turned out well we have to make other prayers. Whatever comes our way by chance is unsteady, and the higher it rises the more liable it is to fall. Furthermore, what is doomed to fall delights no one. So it is inevitable that life will be not just very short but very miserable for those who acquire by great toil what they must keep by greater toil. They achieve what they want laboriously; they possess what they have achieved anxiously; and meanwhile they take no account of time that will never more return. New preoccupations take the place of the old, hope excites more hope and ambition more ambition. They do not look for an end to their misery, but simply change the reason for it. We have found our own public honours a torment, and we spend more time on someone else's. We have stopped labouring as candidates, and we start canvassing for others. We have given up the troubles of a prosecutor, and taken on those of a judge. A man stops being a judge and becomes president of a court. He has grown old in the job of managing the property of others for a salary, and then spends all his time looking after his own. Marius was released from army life to become busy in the consulship. Quintius hastens to get through his dictatorship, but he will be summoned back to it from the plough. Scipio will go against the

Carthaginians before he is experienced enough for such an undertaking. Victorious over Hannibal, victorious over Antiochus, distinguished in his own consulship and a surety for his brother's, if he had not himself forbidden it he would have been set up beside Jupiter. But discord in the state will harass its saviour, and after as a young man he has scorned honours fit for the gods, at length when old he will take delight in an ostentatiously stubborn exile. There will always be causes for anxiety, whether due to prosperity or to wretchedness. Life will be driven on through a succession of preoccupations: we shall always long for leisure, but never enjoy it.

And so, my dear Paulinus, extract yourself from the crowd, and as you have been storm-tossed more than your age deserves, you must at last retire into a peaceful harbour. Consider how many waves you have encountered, how many storms – some of which you have sustained in private life and some you have brought upon yourself in public life. Your virtue has for long enough been shown, when you were a model of active industry: try how it will manage in leisure. The greater part of your life, certainly the better part, has been devoted to the state: take some of your own time for yourself too. I am not inviting you to idle or purposeless sloth, or to drown all your natural energy in sleep and the pleasures that are dear to the masses. That is not to have repose. When you are retired and enjoying peace of mind, you will find to keep you busy more important activities than all those you have performed so energetically up to now. Indeed, you are managing the accounts of the world as scrupulously as you would another person's, as carefully as your own, as conscientiously as the state's. You are winning affection in a job in which it is hard to avoid ill will; but believe me it is better to understand the balance sheet of one's own life than of the corn trade. You must recall that vigorous mind of yours, supremely capable of dealing with the greatest responsibilities, from a task which is certainly honourable but scarcely suited to the happy life; and you must consider that all your youthful training in the liberal studies was not directed to this end, that many thousands of measures of corn might safely be entrusted to you. You had promised higher and greater things of yourself. There will not be wanting men who are completely worthy and hard-working. Stolid pack animals are much more fit for carrying loads than thoroughbred horses: who ever subdued their noble speed with a heavy burden? Consider too how much anxiety you have in submitting yourself to such a weight of responsibility: you are dealing with the human belly. A hungry people neither listens to reason nor is mollified by fair treatment or swayed by any appeals. Quite recently, within a few days after Gaius Caesar died – still feeling very upset (if the dead have feelings) because he saw that the Roman people were still surviving, with a supply of food for seven or at most eight days, while he was building bridges with boats and playing with the resources of the empire – we faced the worst of all afflictions, even to those under siege, a shortage of provisions. His imitation of a mad foreign king doomed in his pride, nearly cost the city destruction and famine and the universal collapse that follows famine. What then must those have felt who had charge of the corn supply, when they were threatened with stones, weapons, fire – and Gaius? With a huge pretence they managed to conceal the great evil lurking in the vitals of the state – and assuredly they had good reason. For certain ailments must be treated while the patient is unaware of them: knowing about their disease has caused the death of many.

You must retire to these pursuits which are quieter, safer and more important. Do you think it is the same thing whether you are overseeing the transfer of corn into granaries, unspoilt by the dishonesty and carelessness of the shippers, and taking care that it does not get damp and then ruined through heat, and that it tallies in measure and weight; or whether you take up these sacred and lofty studies, from which you will learn the substance of god, and his will, his mode of life, his shape; what fate awaits your soul; where nature lays us to rest when released from our bodies; what is the force which supports all the heaviest elements of this world at the centre, suspends the light elements above, carries fire to the highest part, and sets the stars in motion with their proper changes – and learn other things in succession which are full of tremendous marvels? You really should leave the ground and turn your thoughts to these studies. Now while the blood is hot you should make your way with vigour to better things. In this kind of life you will find much that is worth your study: the love and practice of the virtues, forgetfulness of the passions, the knowledge of how to live and die, and a life of deep tranquillity.

Indeed the state of all who are preoccupied is wretched, but the most wretched are those who are toiling not even at their own preoccupations, but must regulate their sleep by another's, and their walk by another's pace, and obey orders in those freest of all things, loving and hating. If such people want to know how short their lives are, let them reflect how small a portion is their own.

So, when you see a man repeatedly wearing the robe of office, or one whose name is often spoken in the Forum, do not envy him: these things are won at the cost of life. In order that one year may be dated from their names they will waste all their own years. Life has left some men struggling at the start of their careers before they could force their way to the height of their ambition. Some men, after they have crawled through a thousand indignities to the supreme dignity, have been assailed by the gloomy thought that all their labours were but for the sake of an epitaph. Some try to adjust their extreme old age to new hopes as though it were youth, but find its weakness fails them in the midst of efforts that overtax it. It is a shameful sight when an elderly man runs out of breath while he is pleading in court for litigants who are total strangers to him, and trying to win the applause of the ignorant bystanders. It is disgraceful to see a man collapsing in the middle of his duties, worn out more by his lifestyle than by his labours. Disgraceful too is it when a man dies in the midst of going through his accounts, and his heir, long kept waiting, smiles in relief. I cannot resist telling you of an instance that occurs to me. Sextus Turannius was an old man known to be scrupulous and diligent, who, when he was ninety, at his own request was given retirement from his office by Gaius Caesar. He then ordered himself to be laid out on his bed and lamented by the assembled household as though he were dead. The house bewailed its old master's leisure, and did not cease its mourning until his former job was restored to him. Is it really so pleasant to die in harness? That is the feeling of many people: their desire for their work outlasts their ability to do it. They fight against their own bodily weakness, and they regard old age as a hardship on no other grounds than that it puts them on the shelf. The law does not make a man a soldier after fifty or a senator after sixty: men find it more difficult to gain leisure from themselves than from the law. Meanwhile, as they rob and are robbed, as they disturb each other's peace, as they make each other miserable, their lives pass without satisfaction, without pleasure, without mental improvement. No one keeps death in view, no one refrains from hopes that look far ahead; indeed, some people even arrange things that are beyond life – massive tombs, dedications of public buildings, shows for their funerals, and ostentatious burials. But in truth, such people's funerals should be conducted with torches and wax tapers, as though they had lived the shortest of lives.

Meditations

BOOK 4

Wherever it is in agreement with nature, the ruling power within us takes a flexible approach to circumstances, always adapting itself easily to both practicality and the given event. It has no favoured material for its work, but sets out on its objects in a conditional way, turning any obstacle into material for its own use. It is like a fire mastering whatever falls into it. A small flame would be extinguished, but a bright fire rapidly claims as its own all that is heaped on it, devours it all, and leaps up yet higher in consequence.

No action should be undertaken without aim, or other than in conformity with a principle affirming the art of life.

Men seek retreats for themselves – in the country, by the sea, in the hills – and you yourself are particularly prone to this yearning. But all this is quite unphilosophic, when it is open to you, at any time you want, to retreat into yourself. No retreat offers someone more quiet and relaxation than that into his own mind, especially if he can dip into thoughts there which put him at immediate and complete ease: and by ease I simply mean a well-ordered life. So constantly give yourself this retreat, and renew yourself. The doctrines you will visit there should be few and fundamental, sufficient at one meeting to wash away all your pain and send you back free of resentment at what you must rejoin.

And what is it you will resent? Human wickedness? Recall the conclusion that rational creatures are born for each other's sake, that tolerance is a part of justice, that wrongdoing is not deliberate. Consider the number of people who spent their lives in enmity, suspicion, hatred, outright war, and were then laid out for burial or reduced to ashes. Stop, then. Or will you fret at your allocation from the Whole? Revisit the alternatives – providence or atoms – and the many indications that the universe is a kind of community. But will matters of the flesh still have their hold on you? Consider that the mind, once it has abstracted itself and come to know its own defining power, has no contact with the movement of the bodily spirit, be that smooth or troubled: and finally remember all that you have heard and agreed about pain and pleasure.

Well then, will a little fame distract you? Look at the speed of universal oblivion, the gulf of immeasurable time both before and after, the vacuity of applause, the indiscriminate fickleness of your apparent supporters, the tiny room in which all this is confined. The whole earth is a mere point in space: what a minute cranny within this is your own habitation, and how many and what sort will sing your praises here!

Finally, then, remember this retreat into your own little territory within yourself. Above all, no agonies, no tensions. Be your own master, and look at things as a man, as a human being, as a citizen, as a mortal creature. And here are two of the most immediately useful thoughts you will dip into. First that *things* cannot touch the mind: they are external and inert; anxieties can only come from your internal judgement. Second, that all these things you see will change almost as you look at them, and then will be no more. Constantly bring to mind all that you yourself have already seen changed. The universe is change: life is judgement.

If mind is common to us all, then we have reason also in common – that which makes us rational beings. If so, then common too is the reason which dictates what we should or should not do. If so, then law too is common to us all. If so, then we are Citizens. If so, we share in a constitution. If so, the universe is a kind of community. In what else could one say that the whole human race shares a common constitution?

From there, then, this common city, we take our very mind, our reason, our law – from where else? Just as the earthy part of me has been derived from some earth, the watery from the next element, the air of my breath from some other source, the hot and fiery from its own origin (for nothing comes from nothing, nor returns to nothing) – so the mind also has its source.

Death, just like birth, is a mystery of nature: first a combination, then a dissolution, of the same elements. Certainly no cause for shame: because nothing out of the order for an intelligent being or contrary to the principle of his constitution.

With such people such an outcome is both natural and inevitable – if you wish it otherwise you are hoping that figs will no longer produce their rennet. In any case remember that in a very brief time both you and he will be dead, and shortly after not even your names will be left.

Remove the judgement, and you have removed the thought 'I am hurt': remove the thought 'I am hurt', and the hurt itself is removed.

What does not make a human being worse in himself cannot make his life worse either: it cannot harm him from outside or inside.

The nature of the beneficial was bound to act thus.

'All's right that happens in the world.' Examine this saying carefully, and you will find it true. I do not mean 'right' simply in the context of cause and effect, but in the sense of 'just' – as if some adjudicator were assigning dues. So keep on observing this, as you have started, and in all that you do combine doing it with being a good man, in the specific conception of 'good man'. Preserve this in every sphere of action.

When someone does you wrong, do not judge things as he interprets them or would like *you* to interpret them. Just see them as they are, in plain truth.

Always have these two principles in readiness. First, to do only what the reason inherent in kingly and judicial power prescribes for the benefit of mankind. Second, to change your ground, if in fact there is someone to correct and guide you away from some notion. But this transference must always spring from a conviction of justice or the common good: and your preferred course must be likewise, not simply for apparent pleasure or popularity.

'Do you possess reason?' 'I do.' 'Why not use it then? With reason doing its job, what else do you want?'

You have subsisted as a part of the Whole. You will vanish into that which gave you birth: or rather you will be changed, taken up into the generative principle of the universe.

Many grains of incense on the same altar. One falls to ash first, another later: no difference.

Within ten days you will be regarded as a god by those very people who now see you as beast or baboon – if you return to your principles and the worship of Reason.

No, you do not have thousands of years to live. Urgency is on you. While you live, while you can, become good.

What ease of mind you gain from not looking at what your neighbour has said or done or thought, but only at your own actions, to make them just, reverential, imbued with good! So do not glance at the black characters either side, but run right on to the line: straight, not straggly.

One who is all in a flutter over his subsequent fame fails to imagine that all those who remember him will very soon be dead – and he too. Then the same will be true of all successors, until the whole memory of him will be extinguished in a sequence of lamps lit and snuffed out. But suppose immortality in those who will remember you, and everlasting memory. Even so, what is that to you? And I do not simply mean that this is nothing to the dead, but to the living also what is the point of praise, other than for some practical aspect of management? As it is, you are losing the opportunity of that gift of nature which does not depend on another's word. So . . .

Everything in any way beautiful has its beauty of itself, inherent and self-sufficient: praise is no part of it. At any rate, praise does not make anything better or worse. This applies even to the popular conception of beauty, as in material things or works of art. So does the truly beautiful need anything beyond itself? No more than law, no more than truth, no more than kindness or integrity. Which of these things derives its beauty from praise, or withers under criticism? Does an emerald lose its quality if it is not praised? And what of gold, ivory, purple, a lyre, a dagger, a flower, a bush?

You may ask how, if souls live on, the air can accommodate them all from the beginning of time. Well, how does the earth accommodate all those bodies buried in it over the same eternity? Just as here on earth, once bodies have kept their residence for whatever time, their change and decomposition makes room for other bodies, so it is with souls migrated to the air. They continue for a time, then change, dissolve, and take fire as they are assumed into the generative principle of the Whole: in this way they make room for successive residents. Such would be one's answer on the assumption that souls do live on.

We should consider, though, not only the multitude of bodies thus buried, but also the number of animals eaten every day by us and other creatures – a huge quantity consumed and in a sense buried in the bodies of those who feed on them. And yet there is room for them, because they are reduced to blood and changed into the elements of air and fire.

How to investigate the truth of this? By distinguishing the material and the causal.

No wandering. In every impulse, give what is right: in every thought, stick to what is certain.

Universe, your harmony is my harmony: nothing in your good time is too early or too late for me. Nature, all that your seasons bring is fruit to me: all comes from you, exists in you, returns to you. The poet says, 'Dear city of Cecrops': will you not say, 'Dear city of Zeus'?

'If you want to be happy', says Democritus, 'do little.' May it not be better to do what is necessary, what the reason of a naturally social being demands, and the way reason demands it done? This brings the happiness both of right action and of little action. Most of what we say and do is unnecessary: remove the superfluity, and you will have more time and less bother. So in every case one should prompt oneself: 'Is this, or is it not, something necessary?' And the removal of the unnecessary should apply not only to actions but to thoughts also: then no redundant actions either will follow.

Try out too how the life of the good man goes for you – the man content with his dispensation from the Whole, and satisfied in his own just action and kind disposition.

You have seen that: now look at this. Do not trouble yourself, keep yourself simple. Someone does wrong? He does wrong to himself. Has something happened to you? Fine. All that happens has been fated by the Whole from the beginning and spun for your own destiny. In sum, life is short: make your gain from the present moment with right reason and justice. Keep sober and relaxed.

Either an ordered universe, or a stew of mixed ingredients, yet still coherent order. Otherwise how could a sort of private order subsist within you, if there is disorder in the Whole? Especially given that all things, distinct as they are, nevertheless permeate and respond to each other.

A black character, an effeminate, unbending character, the character of a brute or dumb animal: infantile, stupid, fraudulent, coarse, mercenary, despotic.

If one who does not recognize the contents of the universe is a stranger in it, no less a stranger is the one who fails to recognize what happens in it. He is a fugitive if he runs away from social principle; blind, if he shuts the eye of the mind; a beggar, if he depends on others and does not possess within him all he needs for life; a tumour on the universe, if he stands aside and separates himself from the principle of our common nature in disaffection with his lot (for it is nature which brings this about, just as it brought you about too); a social splinter, if he splits his own soul away from the soul of all rational beings, which is a unity.

One philosopher has no shirt, one has no book. Here is another half-naked: 'I have no bread', he says, 'but I am faithful to Reason.' But I for my part have all the food of learning, and yet I am not faithful.

Love the art which you have learnt, and take comfort in it. Go through the remainder of your life in sincere commitment of all your being to the gods, and never making yourself tyrant or slave to any man.

Consider, for example, the time of Vespasian. You will see everything the same. People marrying, having children, falling ill, dying, fighting, feasting, trading, farming, flattering, pushing, suspecting, plotting, praying for the death of others, grumbling at their lot, falling in love, storing up wealth, longing for consulships and kingships. And now that life of theirs is gone, vanished.

Pass on again to the time of Trajan. Again, everything the same. That life too is dead.

Similarly, look at the histories of other eras and indeed whole nations, and see how many lives of striving met with a quick fall and resolution into the elements. Above all, review in your mind those you have seen yourself in empty struggles, refusing to act in accord with their own natural constitution, to hold tight to it and find it sufficient. And in this context you must remember that there is proportionate value in our attention to each action – so you will not lose heart if you devote no more time than they warrant to matters of less importance.

Words in common use long ago are obsolete now. So too the names of those once famed are in a sense obsolete – Camillus, Caeso, Volesus, Dentatus; a little later Scipio and Cato, then Augustus too, then Hadrian and Antoninus. All things fade and quickly turn to myth: quickly too utter oblivion drowns them. And I am talking of those who shone with some wonderful brilliance: the rest, once they have breathed their last, are immediately 'beyond sight, beyond knowledge'. But what in any case is everlasting memory? Utter emptiness.

So where should a man direct his endeavour? Here only – a right mind, action for the common good, speech incapable of lies, a disposition to welcome all that happens as necessary, intelligible, flowing from an equally intelligible spring of origin.

Gladly surrender yourself to Clotho: let her spin your thread into whatever web she wills.

All is ephemeral, both memory and the object of memory.

Constantly observe all that comes about through change, and habituate yourself to the thought that the nature of the Whole loves nothing so much as to change one form of existence into another, similar but new. All that exists is in a sense the seed of its successor: but your concept of 'seed' is simply what is put into the earth or the womb – that is very unphilosophic thinking.

Your death will soon be on you: and you are not yet clear-minded, or untroubled, or free from the fear of external harm, or kindly to all people, or convinced that justice of action is the only wisdom.

Look into their directing minds: observe what even the wise will avoid or pursue.

Harm to you cannot subsist in another's directing mind, nor indeed in any turn or change of circumstance. Where, then? In that part of you which judges harm. So no such judgement, and all is well. Even if what is closest to it, your own body, is subjected to knife or cautery, or left to suppurate or mortify, even so that faculty in you which judges these things should stay untroubled. That is, it should assess nothing either bad or good which can happen equally to the bad man or the good: because what can happen to a man irrespective of his life's conformity to nature is not of itself either in accordance with nature or contrary to it.

Think always of the universe as one living creature, comprising one substance and one soul: how all is absorbed into this one consciousness; how a single impulse governs all its actions; how all things collaborate in all that happens; the very web and mesh of it all.

You are a soul carrying a corpse, as Epictetus used to say.

Change: nothing inherently bad in the process, nothing inherently good in the result.

There is a river of creation, and time is a violent stream. As soon as one thing comes into sight, it is swept past and another is carried down: it too will be taken on its way.

All that happens is as habitual and familiar as roses in spring and fruit in the summer. True too of disease, death, defamation, and conspiracy – and all that delights or gives pain to fools.

What comes after is always in affinity to what went before. Not some simple enumeration of disparate things and a merely necessary sequence, but a rational connection: and just as existing things are harmoniously interconnected, so the processes of becoming exhibit no mere succession, but a wonderfully inherent affinity.

Always remember Heraclitus: 'The death of earth is the birth of water; the death of water is the birth of air; the death of air is fire, and back again.' Remember too his image of the man who forgets his way home; his saying that men are at odds with their most constant companion, the Reason which governs all things; that their everyday experience takes them by surprise; that we must not act or speak as if asleep, and sleep brings the illusion of speech and action; and that we should not be like children with their parents, simply accepting what we are told.

Just as if a god told you that you would die tomorrow or at least the day after tomorrow, you would attach no importance to the difference of one day, unless you are a complete coward (such is the tiny gap of time): so you should think there no great difference between life to the umpteenth year and life to tomorrow.

Think constantly how many doctors have died, after knitting their brows over their own patients; how many astrologers, after predicting the deaths of others, as if death were something important; how many philosophers, after endless deliberation on death or immortality; how many heroes, after the many others they killed; how many tyrants, after using their power over men's lives with monstrous insolence, as if they themselves were immortal. Think too how many whole cities have 'died' – Helice, Pompeii, Herculaneum, innumerable others. Go over now all those you have known yourself, one after the other: one man follows a friend's funeral and is then laid out himself, then another follows him – and all in a brief space of time. The conclusion of this? You should always look on human life as short and cheap. Yesterday sperm: tomorrow a mummy or ashes.

So one should pass through this tiny fragment of time in tune with nature, and leave it gladly, as an olive might fall when ripe, blessing the earth which bore it and grateful to the tree which gave it growth.

Be like the rocky headland on which the waves constantly break. It stands firm, and round it the seething waters are laid to rest.

'It is my bad luck that this has happened to me.' No, you should rather say: 'It is my good luck that, although this has happened to me, I can bear it without pain, neither crushed by the present nor fearful of the future.' Because such a thing could have happened to any man, but not every man could have borne it without pain. So why see more misfortune in the event than good fortune in your ability to bear it? Or in general would you call anything a misfortune for a man which is not a deviation from man's nature? Or anything a deviation from man's nature which is not contrary to the purpose of his nature? Well, then. You have learnt what that purpose is. Can there be anything, then, in this happening which prevents you being just, high-minded, self-controlled, intelligent, judicious, truthful, honourable and free – or any other of those attributes whose combination is the fulfilment of man's proper nature? So in all future events which might induce sadness remember to call on this principle: 'this is no misfortune, but to bear it true to yourself is good fortune.'

An unphilosophic but nonetheless effective help to putting death in its place is to run over the list of those who have clung long to life. What did they gain over the untimely dead? At any rate they are all in their graves by now – Caedicianus, Fabius, Julianus, Lepidus, and all others like them who took part in many funerals and then their own. In truth, the distance we have to travel is small: and we drag it out with such labour, in such poor company, in such a feeble body. No great thing, then. Look behind you at the huge gulf of time, and another infinity ahead. In this perspective what is the difference between an infant of three days and a Nestor of three generations?

Always run on the short road: and nature's road is short. Go then for the healthiest in all you say and do. Such a purpose releases a man from the labours of service, from all need to manage or impress.

BOOK 5

At break of day, when you are reluctant to get up, have this thought ready to mind: 'I am getting up for a man's work. Do I still then resent it, if I am going out to do what I was born for, the purpose for which I was brought into the world? Or was I created to wrap myself in blankets and keep warm?' 'But this is more pleasant.' Were you then born for pleasure – all for feeling, not for action? Can you not see plants, birds, ants, spiders, bees all doing their own work, each helping in their own way to order the world? And then you do not want to do the work of a human being – you do not hurry to the demands of your own nature. 'But one needs rest too.' One does indeed: I agree. But nature has set limits to this too, just as it has to eating and drinking, and yet you go beyond these limits, beyond what you need. Not in your actions, though, not any longer: here you stay below your capability.

The point is that you do not love yourself – otherwise you would love both your own nature and her purpose for you. Other men love their own pursuit and absorb themselves in its performance to the exclusion of bath and food: but you have less regard for your own nature than the smith has for his metalwork, the dancer for his dancing, the money-grubber for his money, the exhibitionist for his little moment of fame. Yet these people, when impassioned, give up food and sleep for the promotion of their pursuits: and you think social action less important, less worthy of effort?

How easy it is to drive away or obliterate from one's mind every impression which is troublesome or alien, and then to be immediately in perfect calm.

Judge yourself entitled to any word or action which is in accord with nature, and do not let any subsequent criticism or persuasion from anyone talk you out of it. No, if it was a good thing to do or say, do not revoke your entitlement. Those others are guided by their own minds and pursue their own impulses. Do not be distracted by any of this, but continue straight ahead, following your own nature and universal nature: these two have one and the same path.

I travel on by nature's path until I fall and find rest, breathing my last into that air from which I draw my daily breath, and falling on that earth which gave my father his seed, my mother her blood, my nurse her milk; the earth which for so many years has fed and watered me day by day; the earth which bears my tread and all the ways in which I abuse her.

They cannot admire you for intellect. Granted – but there are many other qualities of which you cannot say, 'but that is not the way I am made'. So display those virtues which are wholly in your own power – integrity, dignity, hard work, self-denial, contentment, frugality,

kindness, independence, simplicity, discretion, magnanimity. Do you not see how many virtues you can
already display without any excuse of lack of talent or
aptitude? And yet you are still content to lag behind. Or
does the fact that you have no inborn talent oblige you
to grumble, to scrimp, to toady, to blame your poor
body, to suck up, to brag, to have your mind in such
turmoil? No, by heaven, it does not! You could have got
rid of all this long ago, and only be charged – if charge
there is – with being rather slow and dull of comprehension. And yet even this can be worked on – unless you
ignore or welcome your stupidity.

One sort of person, when he has done a kindness to
another, is quick also to chalk up the return due to him.
A second is not so quick in that way, but even so he
privately thinks of the other as his debtor, and is well
aware of what he has done. A third sort is in a way not
even conscious of his action, but is like the vine which
has produced grapes and looks for nothing else once it
has borne its own fruit. A horse that has raced, a dog
that has tracked, a bee that has made honey, and a man
that has done good – none of these knows what they
have done, but they pass on to the next action, just as
the vine passes on to bear grapes again in due season.
So you ought to be one of those who, in a sense, are
unconscious of the good they do. 'Yes', he says, 'but this
is precisely what one should be conscious of: because it
defines the social being to be aware of his social action,
and indeed to want his fellow to be aware of it also.'

'True, but you misunderstand the point I am now making: and for that reason you will fall into one of the first categories I mentioned. They too are misled by some sort of plausible logic. But if you want to follow my meaning, don't fear that this will lead you to any deficiency of social action.'

A prayer of the Athenian people:

> Rain, rain, dear Zeus:
> rain on the cornfields
> and the plains of Athens.

Prayer should be thus simple and open, or not at all.

Just as it is commonly said that Asclepius has prescribed someone horse-riding, or cold baths, or walking barefoot, so we could say that the nature of the Whole has prescribed him disease, disablement, loss, or any other such affliction. In the first case 'prescribed' means something like this: 'ordered this course for this person as conducive to his health'. In the second the meaning is that what happens to each individual is somehow arranged to conduce to his destiny. We speak of the fitness of these happenings as masons speak of the 'fit' of squared stones in walls or pyramids, when they join each other in a defined relation.

In the whole of things there is one harmony: and just as all material bodies combine to make the world one body, a harmonious whole, so all causes combine to make Destiny one harmonious cause. Even quite unsophisticated people intuit what I mean. They say: 'Fate brought this on him.' Now if 'brought', also 'prescribed'. So let us accept these prescriptions just as we accept those of Asclepius – many of them too are harsh, but we welcome them in the hope of health.

You should take the same view of the process and completion of the design of universal nature as you do of your own health: and so welcome all that happens to you, even if it seems rather cruel, because its purpose leads to the health of the universe and the prosperity and success of Zeus. He would not bring this on anyone, if it did not also bring advantage to the Whole: no more than any given natural principle brings anything inappropriate to what it governs.

So there are two reasons why you should be content with your experience. One is that this has happened to you, was prescribed for you, and is related to you, a thread of destiny spun for you from the first by the most ancient causes. The second is that what comes to each individual is a determining part of the welfare, the perfection, and indeed the very coherence of that which governs the Whole. Because the complete Whole is maimed if you sever even the tiniest fraction of its connection and continuity: this is true of its constituent parts, and true likewise of its causes. And you do sever something, to the extent that you can, whenever you fret at your lot: this is, in a sense, a destruction.

Do not give up in disgust or impatience if you do not find action on the right principles consolidated into a habit in all that you do. No: if you have taken a fall, come back again, and be glad if most of your actions are on the right side of humanity. And love what you return to. Do not come back to philosophy as schoolboy to tutor, but rather as a man with ophthalmia returns to his sponge and salve, or another to his poultice or lotion. In this way you will prove that obedience to reason is no great burden, but a source of relief. Remember too that philosophy wants only what your nature wants: whereas you were wanting something unnatural to you. Now what could be more agreeable than the needs of your own nature? This is the same way that pleasure trips us: but look and see whether there is not something more agreeable in magnanimity, generosity, simplicity, consideration, piety. And what is more agreeable than wisdom itself, when you reflect on the sure and constant flow of our faculty for application and understanding?

Realities are wrapped in such a veil (as it were) that several philosophers of distinction have thought them altogether beyond comprehension, while even the Stoics think them hard to comprehend. And every assent we may give to our perceptions is fallible: the infallible man does not exist. Pass, then, to the very objects of our experience – how short-lived they are, how shoddy: a catamite, a whore, a thief could own them. Go on now to the characters of your fellows: it is hard to tolerate even the best of them, not to speak of one's difficulty in enduring even oneself.

In all this murk and dirt, in all this flux of being, time,

movement, things moved, I cannot begin to see what on earth there is to value or even to aim for. Rather the opposite: one should console oneself with the anticipation of natural release, not impatient of its delay, but taking comfort in just these two thoughts. One, that nothing will happen to me which is not in accordance with the nature of the Whole: the other, that it is in my control to do nothing contrary to my god and the divinity within me – no one can force me to this offence.

To what use, then, am I now putting my soul? Ask yourself this question on every occasion. Examine yourself. 'What do I now have in this part of me called the directing mind? What sort of soul do I have after all? Is it that of a child? A boy? A woman? A despot? A beast of the field? A wild animal?'

Here is a way to understand what sort of things the majority take to be 'goods'. If you think of the true goods there are – wisdom, for example, self-control, justice, courage – with these in your mind you could not give any credence to the popular saying of 'too many goods to make room', because it will not apply. But bearing in mind what the majority see as goods you will hear and readily accept what the comic poet says as a fair comment. Even the majority can intuit this difference. Otherwise this saying would not both cause offence and rejection, while at the same time we take it as a telling and witty comment on wealth and the privileges of luxury and fame. Go on, then, and ask whether we should value and judge as goods those things which, when we have thought of them, would properly apply to their owner the saying, 'He is so rich, he has no room to shit.'

I am made up of the causal and the material. Neither of these will disappear into nothing, just as neither came to be out of nothing. So every part of me will be assigned its changed place in some part of the universe, and that will change again into another part of the universe, and so on to infinity. A similar sequence of change brought me into existence, and my parents before me, and so back in another infinity of regression. Nothing forbids this assertion, even if the universe is subject to the completion of cycles.

Reason and the art of reasoning are faculties self-determined by their own nature and their own products. They start from the relevant premise and follow the path to the proposed end. That is why acts of reason are called 'right' acts, signifying the rightness of the path thus followed.

One should pay no attention to any of those things which do not belong to man's portion incumbent on him as a human being. They are not demanded of a man; man's nature does not proclaim them; they are not consummations of that nature. Therefore they do not constitute man's end either, nor yet any means to that end – that is, good. Further, if any of these things were incumbent on a man, then it would not have been incumbent on him to disdain or resist them; we would not commend the man who shows himself free from need of them; if these things were truly 'goods', a man who fails to press for his full share of any of them could not be a good man. But in fact the more a man deprives himself of these or suchlike, or tolerates others depriving him, the better a man he is.

Your mind will take on the character of your most frequent thoughts: souls are dyed by thoughts. So dye your own with a succession of thoughts like these. For example: where life can be lived, so can a good life; but life can be lived in a palace; therefore a good life can be lived in a palace. Again: each creature is made in the interest of another; its course is directed to that for which it was made; its end lies in that to which its course is directed; and where its end is, there also for each is its benefit and its good. It follows that the good of a rational creature is community. It has long been shown that we are born for community – or was it not clear that inferior creatures are made in the interest of the superior, and the superior in the interest of each other? But animate is superior to inanimate, and rational to the merely animate.

To pursue the impossible is madness: and it is impossible for bad men not to act in character.

Nothing happens to any creature beyond its own natural endurance. Another has the same experience as you: either through failure to recognize what has happened to him, or in a display of courage, he remains calm and untroubled. Strange, then, that ignorance and pretension should be stronger than wisdom.

Things of themselves cannot touch the soul at all. They have no entry to the soul, and cannot turn or move it. The soul alone turns and moves itself, making all externals presented to it cohere with the judgements it thinks worthy of itself.

In one respect man is something with the closest affinity to us, in that it is our duty to do good to men and tolerate them. But in so far as some are obstacles to my proper work, man joins the category of things indifferent to me – no less than the sun, the wind, a wild animal. These can impede some activity, yes, but they form no impediments to my impulse or my disposition, because here there is conditional commitment and the power of adaptation. The mind adapts and turns round any obstacle to action to serve its objective: a hindrance to a given work is turned to its furtherance, an obstacle in a given path becomes an advance.

Revere the ultimate power in the universe: this is what makes use of all things and directs all things. But similarly revere the ultimate power in yourself: this is akin to that other power. In you too this is what makes use of all else, and your life is governed by it.

What is not harmful to the city does not harm the citizen either. Whenever you imagine you have been harmed, apply this criterion: if the city is not harmed by this, then I have not been harmed either. If on the other hand harm is done to the city, you should not be angry, but demonstrate to the doer of this harm what he has failed to see himself.

Reflect often on the speed with which all things in being, or coming into being, are carried past and swept away. Existence is like a river in ceaseless flow, its actions a constant succession of change, its causes innumerable in their variety: scarcely anything stands still, even what is most immediate. Reflect too on the yawning gulf of past and future time, in which all things vanish. So in all this it must be folly for anyone to be puffed with ambition, racked in struggle, or indignant at his lot – as if this was anything lasting or likely to trouble him for long.

Think of the whole of existence, of which you are the tiniest part; think of the whole of time, in which you have been assigned a brief and fleeting moment; think of destiny – what fraction of that are you?

Another does wrong. What is that to me? Let him see to it: he has his own disposition, his own action. I have now what universal nature wishes me to have now, and I do what my own nature wishes me to do now.

The directing and sovereign part of your soul must stay immune to any current in the flesh, either smooth or troubled, and keep its independence: it must define its own sphere and confine those affections to the parts they affect. When, though, as must happen in a composite unity, these affections are transmitted to the mind along the reverse route of sympathy, then you must not try to deny the perception of them: but your directing mind must not of itself add any judgement of good or bad.

'Live with the gods.' He lives with the gods who consistently shows them his soul content with its lot, and performing the wishes of that divinity, that fragment of himself which Zeus has given each person to guard and guide him. In each of us this divinity is our mind and reason.

Are you angry with the man who smells like a goat, or the one with foul breath? What will you have him do? That's the way his mouth is, that's the way his armpits are, so it is inevitable that they should give out odours to match. 'But the man is endowed with reason,' you say, 'and if he puts his mind to it he can work out why he causes offence.' Well, good for you! So you too are no less endowed with reason: bring your rationality, then, to bear on his rationality – show him, tell him. If he listens, you will cure him, and no need for anger.

Neither hypocrite nor whore.

You can live here in this world just as you intend to live when you have left it. But if this is not allowed you, then you should depart life itself – but not as if this were some misfortune. 'The fire smokes and I leave the house.' Why think this any big matter? But as long as no such thing drives me out, I remain a free man and no one will prevent me doing what I wish to do: and my wish is to follow the nature of a rational and social being.

The intelligence of the Whole is a social intelligence. Certainly it has made the lower for the sake of the higher, and set the higher in harmony with each other. You can see how it has subordinated some creatures, coordinated others, given each its proper place, and brought together the superior beings in unity of mind.

How have you behaved up to now towards gods, parents, brother, wife, children, teachers, tutors, friends, relations, servants? Has your principle up to now with all of these been 'say no evil, do no evil'? Remind yourself what you have been through and had the strength to endure; that the story of your life is fully told and your service completed; how often you have seen beauty, disregarded pleasure and pain, forgone glory, and been kind to the unkind.

Why do unskilled and ignorant minds confound the skilful and the wise? Well, what is the mind of true skill and wisdom? It is the mind which knows the beginning and the end, and knows the Reason which informs all of existence and governs the Whole in appointed cycles through all eternity.

In no time at all ashes or bare bones, a mere name or not even a name: and if a name, only sound and echo. The 'prizes' of life empty, rotten, puny: puppies snapping at each other, children squabbling, laughter turning straight to tears. And Faith, Honour, Justice and Truth 'fled up to Olympus from the wide-wayed earth'.

So what is there left to keep us here, if the objects of sense are ever changeable and unstable, if our senses themselves are blurred and easily smudged like wax, if our very soul is a mere exhalation of blood, if success in such a world is vacuous? What, then? A calm wait for whatever it is, either extinction or translation. And until the time for that comes, what do we need? Only to worship and praise the gods, and to do good to men – to bear and forbear. And to remember that all that lies within the limits of our poor carcass and our little breath is neither yours nor in your power.

You can always ensure the right current to your life if you can first follow the right path – if, that is, your judgements and actions follow the path of reason. There are two things common to the souls of all rational creatures, god or man: they are immune to any external impediment, and the good they seek resides in a just disposition and just action, with this the limit of their desire.

If this is no wrongdoing of mine, nor the result of any wrong done to me, and if the community is not harmed, then why do I let it trouble me? And what is the harm that can be done to the community?

Don't let the impression of other people's grief carry you away indiscriminately. Help them, yes, as best you can and as the case deserves, even if their grief is for the loss of something indifferent: but do not imagine their loss as any real harm – that is the wrong way of thinking. Rather, you should be like the old man in the play who reclaimed at the end his foster-child's favourite toy, never forgetting that it was only a toy. So there you are, broadcasting your pity on the hustings – have you for-gotten, man, what these things are worth? 'Yes, but they are important to these folk.' Is that any reason for you to join their folly?

'There was a time when I met luck at every turn.' But luck is the good fortune you determine for yourself: and good fortune consists in good inclinations of the soul, good impulses, good actions.

BOOK 9

Injustice is sin. When universal Nature has constituted rational creatures for the sake of each other – to benefit one another as deserved, but never to harm – anyone contravening her will is clearly guilty of sin against the oldest of the gods: because universal Nature is the nature of ultimate reality, to which all present existence is related.

Lying, too, is a sin against the same goddess: her name is Truth, and she is the original cause of all that is true. The conscious liar sins to the extent that his deceit causes injustice: the unconscious liar to the extent that he is out of tune with the nature of the Whole and out of order with the nature of the ordered universe against which he fights. And it *is* fighting when he allows himself to be carried in opposition to the truth. He has received the prompts from nature: by ignoring them he is now incapable of distinguishing false from true.

Moreover, the pursuit of pleasure as a good and the avoidance of pain as an evil constitutes sin. Someone like that must inevitably and frequently blame universal Nature for unfair distribution as between bad men and good, since bad men are often deep in pleasures and the possessions which make for pleasure, while the good often meet with pain and the circumstances which cause pain.

Further, anyone who fears pain will also at times be afraid of some future event in the world, and that is immediate sin. And a man who pursues pleasure will not hold back from injustice – an obvious sin. Those who wish to follow Nature and share her mind must themselves be indifferent to those pairs of opposites to which universal Nature is indifferent – she would not create these opposites if she were not indifferent either way. So anyone who is not himself indifferent to pain and pleasure, death and life, fame and obscurity – things which universal Nature treats indifferently – is clearly committing a sin.

By 'universal Nature treating these things indifferently' I mean that they happen impartially by cause and effect to all that comes into being and owes its being to the fulfilment of an original impulse of Providence. Under this impulse Providence set out from a first premise to establish the present order of the universe: she had conceived certain principles of what was to be, and determined generative powers to create substances, transformations, and successive regeneration.

A man of sense and sensitivity would depart the company of men without ever tasting falsehood, pretence of any kind, excess, or pomp. The next best course is at least to sicken of these things before your final breath. Or do you prefer to sit at table with wickedness? Has your experience not yet persuaded you to shun this plague? Because the corruption of the mind is much more a plague than any such contaminating change in the surrounding air we breathe. The latter infects animate creatures in their animate nature: the former infects human beings in their humanity.

Do not despise death: welcome it, rather, as one further part of nature's will. Our very dissolution is just like all the other natural processes which life's seasons bring – like youth and old age, growth and maturity, development of teeth and beard and grey hair, insemination, pregnancy, and childbirth. In the educated attitude to death, then, there is nothing superficial or demanding or disdainful: simply awaiting it as one of the functions of nature. And just as you may now be waiting for the child your wife carries to come out of the womb, so you should look forward to the time when your soul will slip this bodily sheath.

If you want another criterion – unscientific but emotionally effective – you will find it quite easy to face death if you stop to consider the business you will be leaving and the sort of characters which will no longer contaminate your soul. You must not of course take offence at them, rather care for them and tolerate them kindly: but still remember that the deliverance death brings is not deliverance from the like-minded. This alone, if anything could, might pull you back and hold you to life – if you were allowed to live in the company of people who share your principles. But as things are you see how wearisome it is to live out of tune with your fellows, so that you say: 'Come quickly, death, or I too may forget myself.'

The sinner sins against himself: the wrongdoer wrongs himself, by making himself morally bad.

There can often be wrongs of omission as well as commission.

These will suffice: the present certainty of judgement, the present social action, the present disposition well content with any effect of an external cause.

Erase the print of imagination, stop impulse, quench desire: keep your directing mind its own master.

Irrational creatures share in one animate soul, and rational creatures partake in one intelligent soul: just as there is one earth for all the things of earth, and one light to see by, one air to breathe for all of us who have sight and life.

All things which share some common quality tend to their own kind. Everything earthy inclines to earth. Everything watery flows together, and the same with air, so they need physical obstacles to force a separation. Fire rises upwards because of the elemental fire, but is nevertheless so eager to help the ignition of any fire here below that any material which is a little too dry is easily ignited, for the lack of ingredients which hinder combustion.

So too everything which shares in a common intelligent nature tends equally, or yet more so, to its own kind. Proportionate to its superiority over the rest, it is that much readier to mix and blend with its family.

So right from the beginning among the irrational creatures there could be seen hives, flocks, birds rearing their young, a sort of love: already there were animate souls at work there, and in the higher orders an increasingly strong collective bond which is not found in plants or stones or wood. And among the rational creatures there were civic communities, friendships, households, assemblies: and in war treaties and truces. Among yet higher things there exists a sort of unity even at a distance, as with the stars. Thus the upper reaches of the scale of being can effect fellow feeling even when the members are far apart.

Look then at what is happening now. Only the intelligent creatures have now forgotten that urge to be unified with each other: only here will you see no confluence. They may run from it, but nevertheless they are overtaken: such is the power of nature. Look carefully and you will see what I mean. You are more likely to find earth not returning to earth than a man cut off from man.

Man, god, and the universe all bear fruit, each in its own due season. No matter if common use confines the strict sense of 'bearing fruit' to vines and the like. Reason too has its fruit, both universal and particular: other things grow from it which share its own nature.

If you can, show them the better way. If you cannot, remember that this is why you have the gift of kindness. The gods too are kind to such people, and in their benevolence even help them achieve some ends – health, wealth, fame. You can do it too. Or tell me – who is stopping you?

Work. Don't work as a miserable drudge, or in any expectation of pity or admiration. One aim only: action or inaction as civic cause demands.

Today I escaped from all bothering circumstances – or rather I threw them out. They were nothing external, but inside me, just my own judgements.

All things are the same: familiar in experience, transient in time, sordid in substance. Everything now is as it was in the days of those we have buried.

Mere things stand isolated outside our doors, with no knowledge or report of themselves. What then reports on them? Our directing mind.

Good or ill for the rational social being lies not in feeling but in action: just as also his own virtue or vice shows not in what he feels, but in what he does.

A stone thrown in the air: nothing bad for it on the way down or good for it on the way up.

Penetrate into their directing minds, and you will see what sort of critics you fear – and what poor critics they are of themselves.

All things are in a process of change. You yourself are subject to constant alteration and gradual decay. So too is the whole universe.

You should leave another's wrong where it lies.

The termination of an activity, the pause when an impulse or judgement is finished – this is a sort of death, but no harm in it. Turn now to the stages of your life – childhood, say, adolescence, prime, old age. Here too each change a death: anything fearful there? Turn now to your life with your grandfather, then with your mother, then with your [adoptive] father. And as you find many other examples of dissolution, change, or termination, ask yourself: 'Was there anything to fear?' So too there is nothing to fear in the termination, the pause, and the change of your whole life.

Hurry to your own directing mind, to the mind of the Whole, and to the mind of this particular man. To your own mind, to make its understanding just; to the mind of the Whole, to recall what you are part of; to this man's mind, to see whether there is ignorance or design – and at the same time to reflect that his is a kindred mind.

Just as you yourself are a complementary part of a social system, so too your every action should complement a life of social principle. If any action of yours, then, does not have direct or indirect relation to the social end, it pulls your life apart and destroys its unity. It is a kind of sedition, like an individual in a democracy unilaterally resigning from the common harmony.

Children's tantrums and toys, 'tiny spirits carrying corpses' – the Underworld in the *Odyssey* strikes more real!

Go straight to the qualifying cause and examine it separately from the material element. Then establish the maximum time for which this individual thing thus qualified can by its nature subsist.

You have endured innumerable troubles by not leaving your directing mind to do the work it was made for. But enough.

When another blames you or hates you, or people voice similar criticisms, go to their souls, penetrate inside and see what sort of people they are. You will realize that there is no need to be racked with anxiety that they should hold any particular opinion about you. But you should still be kind to them. They are by nature your friends, and the gods too help them in various ways – dreams and divination – at least to the objects of their concern.

The recurrent cycles of the universe are the same, up and down, from eternity to eternity. And either the mind of the Whole has a specific impulse for each individual case – if so, you should welcome the result – or it had a single original impulse, from which all else follows in consequence: and why should you be anxious about that? The Whole is either a god – then all is well: or if purposeless – some sort of random arrangement of atoms or molecules – you should not be without purpose yourself.

In a moment the earth will cover us all. Then the earth too will change, and then further successive changes to infinity. One reflecting on these waves of change and transformation, and the speed of their flow, will hold all mortal things in contempt.

The universal cause is a torrent, sweeping everything in its stream. So, man, what does that mean for you? Do what nature requires at this moment. Start straight away, if that is in your power: don't look over your shoulder to see if people will know. Don't hope for Plato's utopian republic, but be content with the smallest step forward, and regard even that result as no mean achievement. How worthless are these little men in the public eye who think their actions have anything to do with philosophy! They are full of snot. And who will change their views? Without a change of view what alternative is there to slavery – men groaning and going through the motions of compliance? Go on, then, talk to me now of Alexander and Philip and Demetrius of Phalerum. I shall follow them, if they saw the will of universal nature and took themselves to her school. But if they simply strutted a dramatic role, no one has condemned me to imitate them. The work of philosophy is simple and modest. Do not seduce me to pompous pride.

Take a view from above – look at the thousands of flocks and herds, the thousands of human ceremonies, every sort of voyage in storm or calm, the range of creation, combination, and extinction. Consider too the lives once lived by others long before you, the lives that will be lived after you, the lives lived now among foreign tribes; and how many have never even heard your name, how many will very soon forget it, how many may praise you now but quickly turn to blame. Reflect that neither memory nor fame, nor anything else at all, has any importance worth thinking of.

Calm acceptance of what comes from a cause outside yourself, and justice in all activity of your own causation. In other words, impulse and action fulfilled in that social conduct which is an expression of your own nature.

You can strip away many unnecessary troubles which lie wholly in your own judgement. And you will immediately make large and wide room for yourself by grasping the whole universe in your thought, contemplating the eternity of time, and reflecting on the rapid change of each thing in every part – how brief the gap from birth to dissolution, how vast the gulf of time before your birth, and an equal infinity after your dissolution.

All that you see will soon perish; those who witness this perishing will soon perish themselves. Die in extreme old age or die before your time – it will all be the same.

What are the directing minds of these people? What are they set on, what governs their likes and values? Train yourself to look at their souls naked. When they think that their blame will hurt or their praise advantage, what a conceit that is!

Loss is nothing more than change. Universal nature delights in change, and all that flows from nature happens for the good. Similar things have happened from time everlasting, and there will be more such to eternity. So why do you say that everything has always happened for the bad and always will, that all those gods between them have evidently never found any power to right this, so the world is condemned to the grip of perpetual misery?

The rotting of the base material of everything. Water, dust, bones, stench. Again: marble is a mere deposit in the earth, gold and silver mere sediments; your clothing is animal hair, your purple is fish blood; and so on with all else. And the vital spirit is just the same, changing from this to that.

Enough of this miserable way of life, enough of grumbling and aping! Why are you troubled? What is new in this? What is it that drives you mad? The cause? Then face it. Or rather the material? Then face that. Apart from cause and material there is nothing. But you should even now, late though it is, see to your relation to the gods also: make yourself simpler, and better. Three years is as good as a hundred in this quest.

If he did wrong, the harm is to himself. But perhaps he did not do wrong.

Either all things flow from one intelligent source and supervene as in one coordinated body, so the part should not complain at what happens in the interest of the whole – or all is atoms, and nothing more than present stew and future dispersal. Why then are you troubled? Say to your directing mind: 'Are you dead, are you decayed, have you turned into an animal, are you pretending, are you herding with the rest and sharing their feed?'

Either the gods have power or they do not. Now, if they have no power, why pray? If they do have power, why not pray for their gift of freedom from all worldly fear, desire, or regret, rather than for the presence or absence of this or that? Certainly, if the gods can cooperate with men, they can cooperate to these ends.

But you might say: 'The gods have put these things in my own power.' Is it not then better to use your own power in freedom rather than show a servile and supine concern for what you cannot control? And who told you that the gods do not help us even to the ends which lie within our own power? At any rate, pray about these things, and you will see. One man prays: 'How can I sleep with that woman?' Your prayer is: 'How can I lose the desire to sleep with her?' Another prays: 'How can I be rid of that man?' You pray: 'How can I stop wanting to be rid of him?' Another: 'How can I save my little child?' You: 'How can I learn not to fear his loss?' And so on. Give all your prayers this turn, and observe what happens.

Epicurus says: 'In my illness my conversations were not about the sufferings of my poor body, and I did not prattle on to my visitors in this vein, but I continued to discuss the cardinal principles of natural philosophy, with particular reference to this very point, how the mind shares in such disturbances of the flesh while still preserving its calm and pursuing its own good.' He goes on: 'I did not allow the doctors either to preen themselves on any great achievement, but my life continued fine and proper.' An example, then, for you in sickness, if you are sick, and in any other circumstance. All schools agree that you should not abandon philosophy in any eventualities of life, nor join the ignorant chatter of the uneducated layman. Concentrate only on the work of the moment, and the instrument you use for its doing.

Whenever you are offended at someone's lack of shame, you should immediately ask yourself: 'So is it possible for there to be no shameless people in the world?' It is not possible. Do not then ask for the impossible. This person is just one of the shameless inevitably existing in the world. Have the same thought ready for the rogue, the traitor, every sort of offender. The recognition that this class of people must necessarily exist will immediately make you kinder to them as individuals. Another useful thought of direct application is the particular virtue nature has given us to counter a particular wrong. Gentleness is given as the antidote to cruelty, and other qualities to meet other offences. In general, you can always re-educate one who has lost his way: and anyone who does wrong has missed his proper aim and gone astray.

And what harm have you suffered? You will find that none of these who excite your anger has done anything capable of affecting your mind for the worse: and it is only in your mind that damage or harm can be done to you – they have no other existence.

Anyway, where is the harm or surprise in the ignorant behaving as the ignorant do? Think about it. Should you not rather blame yourself, for not anticipating that this man would make this error? Your reason gave you the resource to reckon this mistake likely from this man, yet you forgot and are now surprised that he went wrong.

Above all, when you complain of disloyalty or ingratitude, turn inwards on yourself. The fault is clearly your own, if you trusted that a man of that character would keep his trust, or if you conferred a favour without making it an end in itself, your very action its own and complete reward. What more do you want, man, from a kind act? Is it not enough that you have done something consonant with your own nature – do you now put a price on it? As if the eye demanded a return for seeing, or the feet for walking. Just as these were made for a particular purpose, and fulfil their proper nature by acting in accordance with their own constitution, so man was made to do good: and whenever he does something good or otherwise contributory to the common interest, he has done what he was designed for, and inherits his own.

BOOK 12

All that you pray to reach at some point in the circuit of your life can be yours now – if you are generous to yourself. That is, if you leave all the past behind, entrust the future to Providence, and direct the present solely to reverence and justice. To reverence, so that you come to love your given lot: it was Nature that brought it to you and you to it. To justice, so that you are open and direct in word and action, speaking the truth, observing law and proportion in all you do. You should let nothing stand in your way – not the iniquity of others, not what anyone else thinks or says, still less any sensation of this poor flesh that has accreted round you: the afflicted part must see to its own concern.

If, then, when you finally come close to your exit, you have left all else behind and value only your directing mind and the divinity within you, if your fear is not that you will cease to live, but that you never started a life in accordance with nature, then you will be a man worthy of the universe that gave you birth. You will no longer be a stranger in your own country, no longer meet the day's events as if bemused by the unexpected, no longer hang on this or that.

God sees all our directing minds stripped of their material vessels, their husks and their dross. His contact is only between his own intelligence and what has flowed from him into these channels of ours. If you train yourself to do the same, you will be rid of what so much distracts you. Hardly likely, is it, that one blind to the enveloping flesh will spend his time eyeing clothes, houses, reputation, or any other such trappings and stage scenery?

There are three things in your composition: body, breath, and mind. The first two are yours to the extent that you must take care of them, but only the third is in the full sense your own. So, if you separate from yourself – that is, from your mind – all that others say or do, all that you yourself have said or done, all that troubles you for the future, all that your encasing body and associate breath bring on you without your choice, all that is whirled round in the external vortex encircling us, so that your power of mind, transcending now all contingent ties, can exist on its own, pure and liberated, doing what is just, willing what happens to it, and saying what is true; if, as I say, you separate from this directing mind of yours the baggage of passion, time future and time past, and make yourself like Empedocles' 'perfect round rejoicing in the solitude it enjoys', and seek only to perfect this life you are living in the present, you will be able at least to live out the time remaining before your death calmly, kindly, and at peace with the god inside you.

I have often wondered how it is that everyone loves himself more than anyone else, but rates his own judgement of himself below that of others. Anyway, if a god or some wise tutor appeared at his side and told him to entertain no internal thought or intention which he won't immediately broadcast outside, he would not tolerate this regime for a single day. So it is that we have more respect for what our neighbours will think of us than we have for ourselves.

However was it that the gods, who have ordered all else so well and with such love for men, overlooked this one thing, that some men, the very best of them, those who had conducted, as it were, the most commerce with the divine and reached the closest relation to it through their acts of devotion and their observances – that these men, once dead, should meet perpetual extinction rather than some return to existence?

Now if this is indeed the case, you can be sure that if it should have been otherwise the gods would have made it otherwise: because if that were right, it would also have been possible, and if in accordance with nature, nature would have brought it about. Therefore the fact that it is not otherwise (if indeed that is a fact) should assure you that it ought not to be otherwise. You can see for yourself that in raising this presumptuous question you are pleading a case with god. But we would not enter such debate with the gods if they were not supremely good and supremely just: and if that is so, they would not have let any part of their ordered arrangement of the world escape them through neglect of justice or reason.

Practise even what you have despaired of mastering. For lack of practice the left hand is awkward for most tasks, but has a stronger grip on the bridle than the right – it is practised in this.

How one should be in both body and soul when overtaken by death; the shortness of life; the immensity of time future and past; the feebleness of all things material.

Look at causation stripped bare of its covers; look at the ulterior reference of any action. Consider, what is pain? What is pleasure? What is death? What is fame? Who is not himself the cause of his own unrest? Reflect how no one is hampered by any other; and that all is as thinking makes it so.

The model for the application of your principles is the boxer rather than the gladiator. The gladiator puts down or takes up the sword he uses, but the boxer always has his hands and needs only to clench them into fists.

See things for what they are, analysing into material, cause, and reference.

What liberty man has to do only what god will approve, and to welcome all that god assigns him in the course of nature!

Do not blame the gods: they do no wrong, willed or unwilled. Do not blame men either: all their wrongs are unwilled. No one, then, should be blamed.

How absurd – and a complete stranger to the world – is the man surprised at any aspect of his experience in life!

Either the compulsion of destiny and an order allowing no deviation, or a providence open to prayer, or a random welter without direction. Now if undeviating compulsion, why resist it? If a providence admitting the placation of prayer, make yourself worthy of divine assistance. If an ungoverned welter, be glad that in such a maelstrom you have within yourself a directing mind of your own: if the flood carries you away, let it take your flesh, your breath, all else – but it will not carry away your mind.

The light of a lamp shines on and does not lose its radiance until it is extinguished. Will then the truth, justice, and self-control which fuel you fail before your own end?

Presented with the impression that someone has done wrong, how do I know that this was a wrong? And if it was indeed a wrong, how do I know that he was not already condemning himself, which is the equivalent of tearing his own face?

Wanting the bad man not to do wrong is like wanting the fig-tree not to produce rennet in its figs, babies not to cry, horses not to neigh, or any other inevitable fact of nature. What else can he do with a state of mind like his? So if you are really keen, cure his state.

If it is not right, don't do it: if it is not true, don't say it.

Your impulse on every occasion should be to a complete survey of what exactly this thing is which is making an impression on your mind – to open it out by analysis into cause, material, reference, and the time-span within which it must cease to be.

Realize at long last that you have within you something stronger and more numinous than those agents of emotion which make you a mere puppet on their strings. What is in my mind at this very moment? Fear, is it? Suspicion? Desire? Something else of that sort?

First, nothing aimless or without ulterior reference. Second, no reference to any end other than the common good.

That in a short while you will be nobody and nowhere; and the same of all that you now see and all who are now alive. It is the nature of all things to change, to perish and be transformed, so that in succession different things can come to be.

That all is as thinking makes it so – and you control your thinking. So remove your judgements whenever you wish and then there is calm – as the sailor rounding the cape finds smooth water and the welcome of a waveless bay.

Any one individual activity which comes to an end at the appropriate time suffers no harm from its cessation:

nor has the agent suffered any harm simply because this particular action has ceased. In the same way, then, if the total of all his actions which constitutes a man's life comes to an end at the appropriate time, it suffers no harm from the mere fact of cessation: nor is the agent who brings this series of actions to a timely end exposed to any harm. The time and the term are assigned by nature – sometimes man's own nature, as in old age, but in any case by the nature of the Whole, which through the constant changing of its constituent parts keeps the whole world ever young and fresh.

Now anything which benefits the Whole is always fine and ripe. It follows that for each of us there is certainly no harm in the cessation of life, as there is no shame either – not self-chosen, not damaging to the common interest. Rather there is good, in that it falls in due season for the Whole, thereby both giving and receiving benefit. Thus too a man walks with god's support when his choice and his direction carry him along god's own path.

Three thoughts to keep at hand. *First:* in your own actions, nothing aimless or other than Justice herself would have done; in external happenings either chance or providence is at work, and one should not blame chance or indict providence. *Second:* the nature of each of us from conception to the first breath of soul, and from that first breath to the surrender of our soul; what elements form our constitution and will be the result of our dissolution. *Third:* that if you were suddenly lifted up to a great height and could look down on human activity and see all its variety, you would despise it, because your view would take in also the great surrounding host of spirits who populate the air and the sky; and that, however many times you were lifted up, you would see the same things – monotony and transience. Such are the objects of our conceit.

Jettison the judgement, and you are saved. And who is there to prevent this jettison?

When you fret at any circumstance, you have forgotten a number of things. You have forgotten that all comes about in accordance with the nature of the Whole; that any wrong done lies with the other; further, that everything which happens was always so in the past, will be the same again in the future, and is happening now across the world; that a human being has close kinship with the whole human race – not a bond of blood or seed, but a community of mind. And you have forgotten this too, that every man's mind is god and has flowed from that source; that nothing is our own property, but even our child, our body, our very soul have come from that source; that all is as thinking makes it so; that each of us lives only the present moment, and the present moment is all we lose.

Continually review in your mind those whom a particular anger took to extremes, those who reached the greatest heights of glory or disaster or enmity or any other sort of fortune. Then stop and think: where is it all now? Smoke and ashes, a story told or even a story forgotten. At the same time this whole class of examples should occur to you: Fabius Catullinus in his country house, Lusius Lupus in his town gardens, Stertinius at Baiae, Tiberius in Capri, Velius Rufus – and generally any obsession combined with self-conceit. Think how worthless all this striving is: how much wiser to use the material given you to make yourself in all simplicity just, self-controlled, obedient to the gods. The pride that prides itself on freedom from pride is the hardest of all to bear.

To those who ask, 'Where then have you seen the gods? What conviction of their existence leads you to this worship of them?', I reply first that they are in fact visible to our eyes. Secondly, and notwithstanding, that I have not seen my own soul either, and yet I honour it. So it is with the gods too: from my every experience of their power time after time I am certain that they exist, and I revere them.

The salvation of life lies in seeing each object in its essence and its entirety, discerning both the material and the causal: in applying one's whole soul to doing right and speaking the truth. There remains only the enjoyment of living a linked succession of good deeds, with not the slightest gap between them.

One light of the sun, even though its path is broken by walls, mountains, innumerable other obstacles. One common substance, even though it is broken up into innumerable forms of individual bodies. One animate soul, even though it is broken up into innumerable species with specific individualities. One intelligent soul, even though it appears divided.

Now in all the above the other parts – such as mere breath, or that material which is insensate – have no direct affinity to each other: yet even here a link is formed by a sort of unity and the gravitation of like to like. But the mind has this unique property: it reaches out to others of its own kind and joins with them, so the feeling of fellowship is not broken.

What more do you want? To live on? Or is it to continue sensation and impulse? To wax and then to wane? To make use of your voice, your mind? What in all this strikes you as good cause for regret? But if every one of these objects is contemptible, go on then to the final aim, which is to follow reason and to follow god. To value these other things, to fret at their loss which death will bring, militates against this aim.

What a tiny part of the boundless abyss of time has been allotted to each of us – and this is soon vanished in eternity; what a tiny part of the universal substance and the universal soul; how tiny in the whole earth the mere clod on which you creep. Reflecting on all this, think nothing important other than active pursuit where your own nature leads and passive acceptance of what universal nature brings.

How does your directing mind employ itself? This is the whole issue. All else, of your own choice or not, is just corpse and smoke.

The clearest call to think nothing of death is the fact that even those who regard pleasure as a good and pain as an evil have nevertheless thought nothing of death.

For one whose only good is what comes in its own proper season, who is equally content with a greater or lesser opportunity to express true reason in his actions, to whom it makes no difference whether he looks on this world for a longer or a shorter time – for him even death has no terrors.

Mortal man, you have lived as a citizen in this great city. What matter if that life is five or fifty years? The laws of the city apply equally to all. So what is there to fear in your dismissal from the city? This is no tyrant or corrupt judge who dismisses you, but the very same nature that brought you in. It is like the officer who engaged a comic actor dismissing him from the stage. 'But I have not played my five acts, only three.' 'True, but in life, three acts can be the whole play.' Completion is determined by that being who caused first your composition and now your dissolution. You have no part in either causation. Go then in peace: the god who lets you go is at peace with you.